Selling Leonardo

Selling Leonardo

The Art World's Greatest Scandal

—A Memoir—

An essay on a learned subject oxford Dictionary

ALEX LAFOLLETTE

RESOURCE *Publications* · Eugene, Oregon

Selling Leonardo
The Art World's Greatest Scandal: A Memoir

Resource Publications
An Imprint of Wipf and Stock Publishers
199 W. 8th Ave., Suite 3
Eugene, OR 97401

www.wipfandstock.com

PAPERBACK ISBN: 978-1-6667-6915-9
HARDCOVER ISBN: 978-1-6667-6916-6
EBOOK ISBN: 978-1-6667-6917-3

VERSION NUMBER 040523

For Erin LaFollette.
The adventure of a lifetime.

"The conman's work is always done for him by his victim."
—CHRISTOPHER HITCHENS

Contents

Acknowledgements

This book would not be possible without the enormous amount of support I have received from friends and family. Their guidance supplied me with the ability to put together this work and share it with you all. Writing is an incredibly isolating activity, so having loved ones that I can lean on has given me the strength to pull this off. My wife, Erin LaFollette, has shown not only great support, but tremendous patience with me while I completed this work. This story would simply not come to fruition without her insight. In addition, there are several others that I would like to call out by name who have helped me with this book. Ruby La-Follette, Ben Lewis, Geoff Mitchell, Doug Ray, Kenny Schachter, Stefan Simchowitz, and Stephanie Welniak. Thank you all for your assistance, as well as putting up with my pestering. It means more to me than I could ever properly express.

Maury LaFollette, I wish that you were able to see this.

Introduction

It does not take much to persuade public opinion. It is easy to get an idea in our heads that there are large groups of people who look to change the minds of the masses. But really there is a step before that one, and it usually begins with just a few people. Large committees, governments, board of directors, they all make sweeping changes, but only after an issue has been presented by someone. The attribution of the painting, *Salvator Mundi*, to Leonardo da Vinci did not come from several museums and many art historians. Rather, it came from just a few people. It was only after these individuals made their expeditious claims that art museums and outsider journalists began to parrot those opinions for an attribution. But what happens when the initial assessment was wrong? The *Salvator Mundi* sold for more than $450 million in 2017. Given the circumstances, it may be too late for these few scholars to walk back their original claims. This story is not about power, but rather the few people who light the spark that creates an explosion. If I had one hope for this book, it would be to show the importance of expressing prudence on important matters. As a society, we cannot afford to jump to our own biased conclusions with every news headline we read, or video clip that we see. Afterall, just as with the false attribution to da Vinci for the *Salvator Mundi*, there tends to be just a few people pulling the strings, telling us what to feel and how to think.

Latin for
Savior of the World

Chapter 1: Letter of Acceptance

On October 2nd, 2018, Saudi Arabian journalist, Jamal Khashoggi, entered the Saudi consulate in Istanbul, Turkey and never left there alive. Once inside, he was attacked by fifteen assassins that strangled him to death and dismembered and disposed of his body. World news headlines began questioning who gave the orders for Khashoggi's murder and what the motives were behind it. It did not take long for the blame to shift towards the Saudi Arabian government. Before his death, in June 2017, Khashoggi fled the Kingdom of Saudi Arabia to live in the United States out of fear for his personal safety. He was an outspoken advocate against the Saudi regime and regularly called for reform of the nation. And now with him being out from under Saudi rule, he was able to operate in a nation that promotes free expression, and without the limitations he had before. His enemies wanted him to be forever silenced. Khashoggi entered the consulate in Istanbul to obtain a marriage permit, and once inside he was attacked by several assassins. Due to the nature of the murder, it not only appears to have been premeditated, but also done with the assistance from intelligence services.[1]

NSO Group Technologies created a sophisticated spyware program called Pegasus, which is sold to various national regimes. This technology can break into any electronic device and have complete, yet covert access to whatever device it has targeted. The list of countries known to actively use Pegasus on their own citizens

---

1. Fogel, *Dissident*, 1:11:29.

is staggering. It makes for gaining personal access to whoever they deem to be a threat incredibly easy. A close friend of Khashoggi's, Omar Abdulaziz, another dissident that is critical of the Saudi regime, had Pegasus secretly installed on his phone. This spyware was able to target his private communications with Khashoggi, and evidence shows it was the Saudi Arabian government that hacked his phone.[2] The world's attention continued to remain steadfast on Saudi Arabia, a country that was actively looking to modernize, but still stuck with global scandals involving advanced spyware and brutal assassinations. Saudi Arabia was now in a public relations crisis and needed to look for ways to get out of it.

Several years after the assassination, on June 21st, 2022, I was on my phone checking emails when I noticed an incoming message from the Louvre Museum in Paris. Already convinced it was a formal rejection letter, I opened the email to find it written in French; obviously. So, I did the virtual walk of shame to Google Translate to at least read how they politely declined my application. *We will issue you an authorization*, read part of the message. I read the Louvre's translated email multiple times which was offering me a coveted permit to be one of their official Copyists. Not only that, but when I originally applied for the honor, I specifically asked if I could recreate my own rendition of Leonardo da Vinci's painting, *Saint John the Baptist*. They granted me that request as well. There instantly came an overwhelming firework of emotions in me. Not only did the Louvre issue me this rare permit, but they also allowed me the privilege of copying a painting made by one of the greatest artists to ever live.

The history of Copyists at the Louvre formally goes back to the French Revolution, the day after the beheading of Marie Antoinette. Although there were many prior Copyists who painted there under various kings' rulings, it became an official program in 1793. But it would be the revolutionaries that opened the Louvre up as a public museum for all French citizens. This included allowing anyone who had the desire to paint copies of the works of art in the museum to be able to do so. In the early days of the

2. Shaheen, "They Silenced Khashoggi," line 9.

Louvre, the halls were filled with artists making their own renditions of masterpieces. Eventually, the Louvre saw that the artists were simply taking up too much space and interfering with visitors who wanted to see the original artworks. Because of this, the Louvre began limiting the number of Copyists it allowed in each year and selected them through an extensive application process. The number of Copyists that the Louvre chooses each year ranges between 150–250 people. These artists today cast a wide net of varying backgrounds, men and women, young and old, French citizen, and foreigner. It is difficult to obtain an official Copyist permit from the Louvre. This is due to the combination of thousands of applicants, and the Louvre's strict standards regarding the artistic background and skill level of the artist.

A Copyist is an artist who creates their own copy of another artwork. Most Copyists I have come across tend to stay as close to the original work as possible, while a minority of them may create varying renditions. My own style as an artist is far from realism, so I would fall into that latter category. And when I applied, I did not think that the Louvre would even respond, much less respond with an affirmative. I had already accomplished a good deal as a thirty-one-year-old artist. My work was in the collections of two museums, I was signed to three different art galleries, and I had sold a decent amount of art over the years. Even with a strong background as an artist, I never would have dreamed that the Louvre would give me one of their limited permits. But they did. And they did because of what I had already achieved in the art world. Receiving that permit was one of the most powerful moments of my life. However, I knew that the challenge of preparing to create my rendition of Leonardo da Vinci's, *Saint John the Baptist*, had only just begun.

Several months prior, my wife, Erin, and I had planned a trip to Paris, France. It was a delayed honeymoon as the Covid lockdowns messed up travel plans for many people, including ourselves. We had already been married for a couple of years and had fun vacations to Florida and New York, and around our home state of Oregon. But finally, we were able to book a trip to Paris.

A couple months after purchasing the plane tickets and finalizing where we were staying, I figured I would send in an application for the Copyist program at the Louvre. I always had the mentality of directly asking for what you want. Fear of rejection is not something I had ever really developed. Along with the application, I included the galleries I showed at, as well as the two museums that have collected my work, and then sent it off. After applying for the program, I quite frankly forgot that I ever even applied because it was such a long shot. However, the following week I received a response from them saying that they were accepting me into their historic Copyist program. My heart still races with excitement whenever I recall that day.

Like many people, I had always admired the accomplishments of da Vinci. I had seen his work before at a previous visit to the Louvre and was familiar with his styles. That being said, I not only had to learn more about his artistic process, but I needed to understand who this man was as a person. With receiving the official permit in June, I had just a few months to prepare for this. The Copyist program at the Louvre allows the artists up to 3 months to create their work in the museum. With Erin and I being in Paris for only seven nights, the option of staying for months in France was just not a possibility. The Louvre was accommodating enough to write the permit for one day on Monday, September 26th, 2022. While I technically could have spent the entire day painting my version of *Saint John the Baptist,* I opted to only take up several moments to recreate the work. I wanted the focus of what I painted to capture the essence and core of the work, rather than looking to make a literal depiction. This is not a common practice among Copyists, as they usually stick as true to form as possible. However, I felt like my talents with art lie more in depicting the emotions of subjects, rather than a photographic representation. And plus, the Louvre Museum was approving of my proposal anyways, so there really wasn't anyone left to justify my vision to.

The true work had now begun. To fully understand just what da Vinci's technique and thought process was, I had to immerse myself into his world. Over the next several months I read five books, totaling well over 2,500 pages. In addition, I read countless articles, spent hours listening to various lectures on Leonardo, and watched several documentaries. Also, a local science museum, Oregon Museum of Science and Industry (OMSI), conveniently had a Leonardo exhibition that featured a couple original drawings of his from the Codex Atlanticus folio. I also created over two hundred sketches of the *Saint John the Baptist* painting. I immersed myself in research and practice to be adequately prepared. Over those few months I formed an obsession with the polymath and the way he went about his world. His art creations were viewed by him in the same way he viewed the sciences. He was critical of the world around him and did not close his mind off to the possibilities of how something could come about.

A person that I leaned on for guidance was my wife, Erin LaFollette. She carries a tremendous amount of insight and I think that she has a better eye for art than I do. I regularly consult her with the art that I make which usually involves the question, *do you think that this is a finished painting?* Her neutrality when it comes to the art that I make has helped me to push the boundaries of expression, and to see where my creative outlets can take me. Erin's understanding of art has also helped guide us with our own art collecting. Neither of us are trust fund babies and have had to financially fight our way through life. Fortunately, both of us have decent jobs which has allowed us to branch out into the world of collecting art. Buying original prints from well-known artists is a passion that the both of us have taken on over the years, and it is Erin's insight for art that drives our collection. It is also important for us that we have a dialogue with museums and to build our legacy together. One of the ways we have done this is by donating art to museums. The arts are something that hit at both of our cores, and we couldn't imagine a life without being immersed in it. Erin has also taken on important projects with well-regarded museums, such as the Louvre Museum in Paris, that has earned her recognition and certificates because of the work she has done for them. We talk about how we live in a type of *Golden Age* for what we do in the arts. However, we also refer to how much of a circus it all can be sometimes.

To further prepare for my Copyist work, I reached out to three of the world's top Leonardo da Vinci scholars for assistance. Dr. Martin Kemp (Oxford University), Dr. Carmen Bambach (Head Curator at The Metropolitan Museum of Art in New York City), And Dr. Frank Zöllner (Leipzig University). Their generosity to answer my questions and help further develop my insight into the workings of Leonardo da Vinci is something that was incredibly beneficial. For example, Dr. Carmen Bambach was able to stress to me that the painting *Saint John the Baptist* was most likely a commissioned work of art for private devotional prayer. This added to the intimacy of this artwork, and its daring nature of depicting a Catholic saint in such a sensual way. Zöllner and Kemp expressed to me their views of the strong authenticity of this painting being done by Leonardo. Kemp even went as far in telling me that *Saint John the Baptist* can be attributed to da Vinci just as much as the *Mona Lisa* can be attributed to him. Having the support of these three leading scholars enhanced my artistic process and understanding of how to go about my rendition. These art experts that helped me with my Copyist work were also previously pulled into what is now known as the greatest art scandal of all time.

Chapter 2: Buried Treasure

The thought of discovering a long-lost masterpiece in your attic crosses the mind from time to time. We all have heard the stories of someone cleaning out their grandparents' home only to find a Rembrandt tucked away between a plastic vase and some firewood. A financial jackpot and a major story on world news outlets quickly follows. These discoveries, although rare, do happen. Important art has been found in people's homes, sometimes with the owner never being aware of what was in their possession. Leonardo da Vinci had a frantic mind and moved from one project to the next, while seemingly only creating a small number of paintings during his lifetime. A decent percentage of those paintings are not even fully attributed to him, like the *Madonna of the Yarnwinder (The Buccleuch Madonna)*. The thought of discovering a painting by a famous artist who did not create many works can create quite the desire. It also makes it next to impossible.

Minnie Stanfill Kuntz and her husband, Warren Kuntz, worked in New Orleans in the furniture business together. They also regularly travelled to Europe over the years with one another. In 1958, they bought the *Salvator Mundi* painting from the estate of Sir Francis Cook for a mere forty-five pounds. Originally it was described as having been by one of Leonardo's students, with no attribution to da Vinci. This *Salvator Mundi* was heavily overpainted and the canvas itself was badly damaged. There was such aging on it that it had a dark appearance. This is probably what had helped make the painting go relatively unnoticed for so long. The painting would live with them for the rest of their lives. Then it was inherited by their nephew, Basil Clovis Hendry Sr., in 1987. After the death of Hendry Sr. the *Salvator Mundi* then went into the possession of his daughter, Susan Hendry Tureau. She put it up for sale in the state of Louisiana at the St. Charles Gallery Auction House in 2005. It sold for about $1,175.[1]

Before this sale of the *Salvator Mundi*, the painting was hung up on the wall in the family's home. None of them could have guessed that someone would later attribute this work to da Vinci. There are thousands of paintings that have survived over the years that were in the ownership of European royalty, and for the most part, these paintings tend to go unnoticed. Sometimes minimal attention is paid to these works because they were done by people who are now deemed as less important artists. Other paintings just do not have enough records for art experts to make an educated claim as to which artist even created it. It is not to say that attribution to certain artworks cannot change over time because they most certainly do. Researchers are constantly gathering as much information as they can about works of art to help gain a better understanding of it. Sifting through old letters and sketchbooks has been critical to understanding the creator of particular works.

In October 2022, art scholars concluded that four paintings that were originally attributed to the artist, Johannes Vermeer, were deemed to have not been made by him. One of these paintings was the famous, *Girl with a Flute*. The news had rocked the art world as our very understanding of who Vermeer was, and the techniques he used, were now under heavy scrutiny.[2] Vermeer was a Dutch artist during the Baroque Period, born a little more than a hundred years after the death of da Vinci. He did not produce a wide range of work, but the paintings he did create have astounded people over the generations. Arguably his most famous painting, *Girl with a Pearl Earring*, painted in 1665, highlights female beauty and youth, and shows his methodic artistic process. The painting underwent a successful restoration in 1994 that was able to bring out the subtle and intimate gaze of the woman. As talented and

1. Blostein, Libetti, and Crow, "$450 Million da Vinci," lines 10–15.
2. Small, "Actually an Imitator," line 3.

innovative as Vermeer was, his students were also able to imitate his style well enough for four of his paintings to no longer be attributed to him.

Major artworks thought to have been lost have also come back into existence over the years. A painting titled, *The Adoration of the Magi*, painted from 1632–1633 by Rembrandt Harmenszoon van Rijn, known by most as just Rembrandt, was rediscovered in Italy in 2016. The owners took it in for restoration, not knowing who the true artist of the work was. During the restoration process it was shown to be an authentic work by Rembrandt. The family who owned this painting believed it to just be a copy and had no idea that it was the real thing. Then in 2021, the French Academy of the Villa Medici in Rome, with support of the Fondazione Patrimonio Italia (FPI), gave the official nod of approval regarding its authenticity.[3] Much of Rembrandt's art has unfortunately been lost over time, so discovering a great work of art by him is very important. The painting is quintessential of Rembrandt's style, such as how he uses darker shades to stress the importance of the figures. He depicts Jesus as a baby, but from afar, and shows the human nature of this little child. The painting also shows a gentler praise coming from those who have come to see the young prophet.

As for the *Salvator* Mundi, two people joined together to buy the painting from the 2005 auction, Alexander Parish and Robert Simon. Simon, an Old Masters specialist, and Parish, a New York based art dealer, must have believed that there was something special about this painting. But even with consulting experts regarding the hand behind the work, they could not know for sure who might have created this until the overpainting was removed. When viewing the artwork, you can see that it was worked on by other artists over the centuries, and that the canvas was in bad shape. Gaining judgements on the art piece in that initial state was not going to provide them many answers. What mattered most was what was underneath the overpainting. Bringing the *Salvator Mundi* down to its most foundational layer could provide the necessary clues as to who made this. Now, the thought of a long-lost

3. Escalante, "Long Lost Rembrandt," lines 2–5.

Leonardo that comes up at a small auction house in the American South sounds like a too good to be true story. And Parish and Simon ended up putting in significant effort to turn this into a major financial triumph for themselves and others. In my opinion, I do not think that Parish nor Simon thought they had simply bought a cheap painting. It seems to me that they always thought bigger.

As this story of the *Salvator Mundi* progresses, it is important to remember that major art discoveries do happen. While these findings are overall a rare occurrence, there are at least a couple stories like this in the news every year. An example of this is when a painting by Gustav Klimt titled, *Portrait of a Lady (1916–1917)* was found in 2019 after having been lost for twenty-three years. The painting was stolen but then discovered by the gardeners of the Ricci Oddi Modern Art, which is the same gallery that it was taken from.[4] And in addition to this, paintings will gain attribution, and others will lose its attribution. There have been many cases which even the artists themselves have been taken to court because of their own declaration of not having created a piece of art. This happened to Peter Doig in 2016 when he said he did not paint a particular landscape. Doig won that court case the same year.[5] Kelly Crow, a friendly acquaintance of mine, and well-respected art market reporter, congratulated me on my Copyist work and my findings regarding the *Salvator Mundi*. This notorious painting is a constant presence in the art world. Parish and Simon buying an ancient work done by a famous artist for $1,175 is not impossible. It does, however, put the pressure on them for coming up with a reason why they think it was painted by Leonardo. The greater the claim, the greater the need for evidence.

4. Iqbal and Jonze, "Art Heists," line 4.
5. Limbong, "He Didn't Paint This," lines 8–9.

Chapter 3: To Rebuild

The Last Supper, one of da Vinci's greatest masterpieces, was created in less than ideal conditions. The main problem regarding this is that the fresco is in a place that suffers from high humidity. Paint had almost immediately began flaking off once it was completed and this continues to be a problem to this day. The first attempted restoration took place in the 1700's, and many more followed. A recent, and vigorous restoration of *The Last Supper* began in 1978 and took twenty-one years. Conservationists focused on removing dirt from the fresco while creating a climate-controlled environment for the artwork. Watercolor was the medium of choice for filling in the gaps of the imagery and looks to me like that medium was chosen to not clash with the aging, original paint. Several critics had disapproving reviews of the multi-decade transformation that included the complaint of mismatched colors and strange facial shapes. Art conservationists tried to save an essential piece of art history, while also attempting to structure a better context for the old mural. Restoration is both difficult and essential work.

Art restoration has been practiced for centuries. It is a vital piece to the arts as it keeps our conversation with the work going. As with anything else, art ages with time. If you make a painting and do not take proper steps to conserve it, then in a few decades that image will look duller. Ancient Greek and Roman statues were usually painted in bright, vibrant colors, and those colors have faded over the years. The *Mona Lisa* is the same as well. What once had the appearance of lush blue and earthy browns, has slowly

..ted over the centuries. The Louvre has taken respectable measures to slow the aging process of the painting. Many museums around the world have conservation departments equipped with their own laboratories to work in. The overall goal of any art restorer is to prevent the work of art from aging, and to delicately add back in what the original artist had created. Restorers are also sensitive to not add more than only the necessary amount of paint to preserve as much of the original as possible.

Bad art restoration easily makes news headlines. It's amusing to see an unknown, irrelevant artwork be restored, only to have its restoration be hideous. Who could forget the 16th century *Saint George* painting in the Church of San Miguel de Estella, Navarre, Spain? The work went from a dirty face to essentially being covered in makeup. Or the Elías García Martinez's, *Ecce Homo* located in the Sanctuary of Mercy Church, Borja, Spain? The painting of the face went from appearing aged, to looking like a rabid monkey. The humor tends to go away when dealing with well-known artworks that are considered important. Examples of these types of restorations include both Leonardo da Vinci's, *Saint John the Baptist* and the 1503 painting, *The Virgin and Child with Saint Anne.* Much more is on the line when restorers are handling art of this caliber. Diane Modestini, who arguably is one of the greatest restorers to ever live, restored the *Salvator Mundi.* She was also the first person to attribute the painting to Leonardo... after she had begun restoring it.

Alexander Parish and Robert Simon brought the painting to Dianne Modestini wrapped inside a garbage bag, on April 27th 2005.[1] Modestini knew that she had to first begin by removing the overpainting to see what lay behind it. Using acetone, mineral spirits, and a cotton swab, she patiently took off the resin and additional paint added to it over the years to bring it back to its original form.[2] This delicate process is time consuming and takes a seasoned professional to be able to successfully accomplish such a thing. Irresponsibly using materials like acetone on a painting

1. Koefoed, *The Lost Leonardo*, 7:28.
2. Modestini, "Condition and Restoration," line 4.

can easily ruin the entire thing. Initially, she did not believe it to be a Leonardo because she was still cleaning it.[3] It appears she was primarily focused on properly using the cleaning material on this very old painting so as not to ruin it. The process for this had to have been arduous. The people who attribute this painting to da Vinci say that it went undiscovered for so long purely because of the vast amount of additional paint previously added to it.[4]

Dianne Modestini already had an impressive art background by the time the painting was brought to her. In 1968 she graduated from Columbia University, and then went to Florence, Italy to study Italian and Drawing at the Academia di Belle Arti. She then earned her M.A. and Certificate of Advanced Study in Art Conservation. She also studied mural conservation at the International Center for the Conservation of Cultural Property in Rome. Between 1974 and 1987, she was the Conservator of Paintings at the Metropolitan Museum of Art, before opening a private practice for art conservation with her husband that same year in 1987. The following year she began teaching at New York University's Conservation Center of the Institute of Fine Arts.[5] Modestini has devoted her life to the arts and has the credentials to prove it. It makes perfect sense as to why Parish and Simon wanted her assistance with figuring out the artist behind this painting. If Modestini can make one big claim about the artwork, then Parish and Simon would at least have something to go off. But first, she must finish the cleaning.

During the cleaning process, Modestini noticed something interesting about the *Salvator Mundi's* right thumb. A pentimento. A pentimento is a mistake by an artist, and then the correction that they make over it. In other words, it is the underpainting of how the artist initially envisioned the work, before changing their mind and painting something different on top of it. Dianne Modestini noticed the pentimento of the right thumb and that the artist originally intended it to be at a different position than what

3. Koefoed, *The Lost Leonardo*, 9:38.
4. Koefoed, *The Lost Leonardo*, 5:41.
5. New York University, "Dianne Modestini," lines 1–4.

it was ultimately presented as. According to Modestini, this was a sign that the painting was created by a master artist, not a student. Her reasoning is that a student would copy a painting exactly as presented and would not make corrections. Upon completion of the cleaning, Dianne Modestini and the owners of the painting said that a main reason for attributing it to Leonardo da Vinci was the pentimento, and the lips having a similar appearance to the *Mona Lisa*.[6]

Locating a pentimento can be used as a minor level of evidence regarding attribution. Art students make mistakes. And it would be reasonable that a student would create a pentimento not only for their own work, but also for ones they are copying. I reached out to Ben Lewis, an art critic who wrote a book on the *Salvator Mundi* titled, *The Last Leonardo: The Secret Lives of the World's Most Expensive Painting*. He confirmed to me that students certainly use pentimento in their works. In addition, I know this as being an artist that there is hardly a painting I make in which there is not a mistake I need to adjust for. Sometimes this includes needing a pentimento. This one finding alone is not enough to show that it is by a master artist, and not a student. In addition, there are several high-level artists who could have painted the *Salvator Mundi* that were not da Vinci. Pentimento does not equal Leonardo. As for the smile, there are minor similarities such as the subtle shading and blending of colors. But in general, the mouth of Christ simply does not reflect the mouth of *Mona Lisa*.

In addition to the overpainting, the panel needed to be repaired due to aging. It was also the victim of many poor restoration treatments over several hundred years. Dianne Modestini would have Monica Griesbach fix this panel, and the project lasted from December 2005 to September 2006. Griesbach used various items from isinglass glue to a B-72 acrylic resin to help preserve it from humidity changes and aging.[7] A key point to note is that the painting was done on walnut wood, which was in fact a preferred panel for Leonardo. The complication from this is that there is a

6. Vitkine, *Savior for Sale*, 9:51.
7. Modestini, "Condition and Restoration," lines 10–15.

large knot in the wood, and as time went on, the canvas split apart because of it. Da Vinci did not do any other paintings with a knot in the wood of the canvas. A perfectionist like Leonardo would discard a panel like this one instead of painting on it. The type of artist that might have used a piece of wood with a knot in it, however, would have been a student. So, while Modestini claims that the pentimento, the lips, and the type of wood for the canvas points to da Vinci, the reality is that it points to a student.

After the overpainting was removed and the panel repaired, the *Salvator Mundi* was then in what is called its *cleaned state*. Many gaps and chipped parts are now visible, and it did not really look that impressive at all. Not much of the original paint was even left. Modestini then began to add paint to the *Salvator Mundi*. Now, a controversy that arises here is why wouldn't the owners of the painting leave it in its present, *cleaned state*? After-all, that is the remaining original work. It is of my opinion that the owners desired to put this painting up for sale with it looking like a well-preserved Leonardo, and not a trainwreck. More of the conspiratorial minded people could say that the restoration was done to hide areas of the painting that show it was not painted by Leonardo. I would not rule something like that out. Nevertheless, Modestini embarked on filling in the gaps with paint. To fill in the gaps she used *Talen's Rembrandt Retouching Varnish* (15% Polycy-clohexanone in a white spirit) and a particular mix of putty that contained a combination of rabbit skin glue, calcium sulphate, and China clay.[8] Modestini painted in the missing parts and looked to leave as much of the original paint as she possibly could.

The painting left her possession in 2008 when it was put on display in London. It then went back to her in 2010 for more res-torations as she felt it was not fully complete. Modestini made her final retouches in 2017, right before the painting was sold in the most notorious art sale of all time. The last retouches she made to the *Salvator Mundi* were the lips.[9] This is controversial because it is one of the main areas she said convinced her that it was made

8. Modestini, "Condition and Restoration," line 24

9. Modestini, "Condition and Restoration," line 37.

by Leonardo. Why re-paint what was deemed as evidence for attribution? This painting had an enormous amount of overpainting on it. And then once removed, there appeared substantial damage, and significant problems with the canvas. Even if this artwork was done by Leonardo, which it was not, there was not much left of the original painting anyways. Leading da Vinci scholar, Frank Zöllner, publicly claimed that the restored *Salvator Mundi* looks much more like a Leonardo after Modestini had worked on it than it did in its original state.[10] After a claim such as this, it should go without saying that Zöllner does not attribute the *Salvator Mundi* to da Vinci. He attributes it instead to Leonardo's Workshop.[11] The restoration of this artwork concludes with the part of the painting that convinced Modestini most of the attribution, the lips.

Frank Zöllner was one of the da Vinci scholars that helped me prepare for my Copyist work at the Louvre. Over the years he had cultivated a vast amount of knowledge regarding the polymath and was able to contextualize da Vinci's work to be better understood. Some of his books include reviewing da Vinci's paintings and drawings and are all matched with extensive notes. One of the many reasons as to why attribution of the *Salvator Mundi* is so controversial is because paintings currently attributed to da Vinci have also had their authorship questioned. Da Vinci kept great notes, just not great records for his paintings. So, for me to gain a better sense of the *Saint John the Baptist* painting, I asked Zöllner about its attribution. He was direct in his response about my question and said that this painting is very much by the hand of Leonardo da Vinci. No studio participation, and no overpainting throughout the years. *Saint John the Baptist* carries a unique intensity to it, and it directly reflects the other paintings, and intricate drawings of da Vinci. It is a truly magnificent painting with no faults, while the *Salvator Mundi* is a total disaster.

---

10. Koefoed, *The Lost Leonardo*, 27:50.

11. Zöllner, *Leonardo*, 440.

Chapter 4: Baptism

In Christian theology, John the Baptist is the one who baptized Jesus Christ in the Jordan River. Many Christian theologians believe John was related to Jesus in some manner, likely as a cousin. However, the exact relationship is not known, as the Bible does not explicitly state a connection. The Baptist is also thought of as a gaunt figure that wanders alone through the desert, surviving off honey and locusts. As with many passages throughout the Bible, there are conflicting stories as to why John was murdered. What they all share is that John is beheaded under orders from Herod. For example, in the *Book of Mark*, Herod reluctantly orders the beheading of John after a dancing woman requests it of him. While in the *Book of Matthew*, Herod is eager for, and personally desires John's decapitation. Artists throughout the years have done various interpretations of John the Baptist. Many of them depict John according to the descriptions in the gospels, such as having dirty hair, a frail body, and wearing camel hair for clothes. The Catholic Church holds John the Baptist in the league of the Saints and essentially all other Christian denominations hold him in high regard as well. He is also a key figure in other religions, such as Islam and Mandaeism. It is worth mentioning that Mandaeism is possibly the first official religion to practice the ceremony of baptism.

Hieronymus Bosch, a Dutch/Netherlandish artist, created an oil painting of John the Baptist in 1489 titled, *St. John the Baptist in the Wilderness*. The painting depicts The Baptist with long hair and a beard, dressed in robes. He is laying down but still awake, and his face shows a bored expression. I think that there is a kind of comedic element to this painting because if someone was wandering the desert alone, it would not take long for boredom to set in. There is even a lamb painted in front of John, which is in reference to Jesus being the Lamb of God. However, John doesn't even seem to be that interested in the lamb either. Bosch does not depict John as a strong figure, or even a handsome one. Instead, he paints him as someone with a lot of time on his hands while counting the minutes for Christ's grand appearance. When this painting was created, Leonardo da Vinci had already long been studying the human body, including real skulls. Da Vinci would focus as much as he could on human anatomy for the sake of the sciences, and this was reflected in his anatomically correct paintings. This will be shown clearly in his version of *Saint John the Baptist*.

Caravaggio completed at least eight known paintings of John the Baptist. These paintings of the Catholic Saint were each depicted in various ways. However, some features he consistently incorporated was to have John be relatively thin with long, brown hair. In addition to these eight paintings, he made three other paintings that depict the beheading of John the Baptist. One of these paintings titled, *Salome with the Head of John the Baptist*, is currently in the collection of the National Gallery in London. Painted around 1607/1610, almost a hundred years after the death of da Vinci, incorporates all of Caravaggio's famous techniques. Dark background with heavy dark shading, overt facial expressions, and figures with a confident movement about them. All we can see of The Baptist in this painting is his cut off head hovering over a plate, with another man holding it up by its hair. It is gruesome. The lifeless head shows the face of someone who spent his years in prayer and intense fasting. This painting is brutal and pulls out the barbarism of his murder in the gospels.

Instead of depicting John the Baptist as being frail, manic, or bored, Leonardo da Vinci painted him as a homoerotic sex symbol. The painting has an all-black background, with John positioned in the middle of the canvas. The head tilts slightly to his right while his left hand lightly cradles a thin, but tall cross. His left index finger points to the center of his chest, and his right arm forms a near

45-degree angle. John's right index finger points upwards towards the heavens. Leonardo paints long, but elegantly curled hair that dangles down the right side of his back. Also, the hair partially lays on the front part of the left side of his chest. The eyes are cartoonish and almond shaped, and stares straight ahead at you. Apart from being wrapped in fur that barely covers his groin area, he is naked. There is a long, strong nose of perfect proportion. And the painting gives off a mystical nature about it as the viewer cannot tell if John is appearing or disappearing as a holy apparition. Da Vinci depicts John as healthy, happy, and well fed. It was the last painting he ever made.

Consensus regarding the dating of this painting is around 1513–1516, and some scholars believe the painting was worked on until 1517. Leonardo passed away in 1519. Nevertheless, there is no credible argument that *Saint John the Baptist* was not the last painting that the polymath created. The provenance of the artwork is solid, as it remained in royal collections over the years with minimal change of hands. Most scholars agree that the painting came into the possession of Salai, one of his students, following the death of da Vinci. It then became a part of the Louvre's permanent collection immediately following the French Revolution. Since the creation of this painting, many followers and admirers of Leonardo have created their own versions. The artist known as Giampietrino (1495–1549) was a follower of Leonardo's and copied his techniques. This was expressed in a painting of John the Baptist that was completed after da Vinci's death, in which he is also shown with very soft, feminine features.

The model for Leonardo's *Saint John the Baptist* appears to be his student, Salai. There is also strong evidence that the two were romantically involved. In da Vinci's notebooks, a drawing has been found depicting Salai as *John the Baptist* for the painting, except instead of a fur robe, he has an exposed erection. This drawing, coupled with the fact that there are essentially no female nude sketches in his notebooks, helps to make this case of the two being lovers. Also found in the notebooks are drawings of penises with legs crawling towards what was shown as Salai's buttocks.

Furthermore, there is a nude version of the *Mona Lisa* done in charcoal that came out of Leonardo's workshop. Salai looks to be the model in that painting as well. Scholars agree that this drawing was created by a left-handed artist, which can make for evidence that it was executed by Leonardo da Vinci. This nude version of the *Mona Lisa* depicts Salai with developed, exposed female breasts. The rest of the painting remains very similar to that of the *Mona Lisa*. This charcoal drawing is referred to as the *La Jaconde Nue*.

Salai was both an artist and student of Leonardo's, joining his studio as an assistant at ten years of age. Leonardo would make disparaging remarks about Salai, like calling him a thief and a glutton. Da Vinci also wrote that Salai stole from him at least half a dozen times. Despite this, Salai lived with Leonardo for more than twenty-five years. After Leonardo's passing in France, it was Salai that was left with much of his belongings, including his art.[1] By training as an artist in da Vinci's workshop, Salai went from being a young troublemaker to at least an older troublemaker who could make decent paintings. In addition to training as an artist and acting as a model in the studio, Salai was predominantly known as Leonardo's assistant. While little is known of the relationship between Salai and Leonardo, we can gather through the paintings and drawings, and the close time spent together, that this relationship was sexual in nature. Later on in life, Salai married a woman in 1523 but would die from a crossbow duel less than a year later.[2]

Over the years people have suggested that maybe Salai was the model for the *Mona Lisa*, as the facial features are certainly similar. And there are other artworks, like the *La Joconde Nue*, that clearly represent him as the *Mona Lisa*. However, we do know now that the *Mona Lisa* is a depiction of the wife of a wealthy merchant. It is plausible that since Leonardo worked on the *Mona Lisa* for so long that he could have used Salai as inspiration for the work. What is clear is that Salai was the model for da Vinci's *Saint John the Baptist*. All the paintings, and various drawings, we have of Salai show that this art piece was in fact of him. Leonardo da Vinci

---

1. Stern, *Queers in History*, 276.
2. Hettie, "Leonardo da Vinci Loved," lines 7–12.

did not opt to depict John the Baptist as a gaunt figure, wandering in meditative prayer through the desert. He wanted to instead show one of the holiest figures in Western religion as his own lover. Da Vinci did not want to depict a narrative scene of John, such as his beheading. He also did not want to show John in the same manner other artists had already done. Instead, he painted a figure that was revolutionary. Leonardo painted a man that smiles at the viewer, telling us all that he knows something that we do not.

Chapter 5: Icon

Da Vinci scholar, Annalisa Di Maria, discovered a drawing in 2020 that may have been created by the polymath. It could also upend the attribution of the *Salvator Mundi* to Leonardo.[1] The drawing is most likely a preparatory sketch for a Salvator Mundi but has significant differences between that and the painting in question. It was done in Leonardo's signature three-quarters view and has many similarities to the other techniques he used. This depiction of Jesus has his head slightly turned, even leveled eyes, and a strong jawline. Christ's hair in this drawing is intricately free flowing. The lips are steady and the gaze is powerful. This red-chalk drawing has a much more powerful presence than the *Salvator Mundi* that is wrongfully attributed to Leonardo da Vinci. There are many rules that needed to be followed for a Renaissance painting, particularly when dealing with a subject matter like a Salvator Mundi. However, beauty and skill were never optional when creating a work of art. As of 2023, the jury is still out if this drawing was completed by Leonardo.

The idea of a Salvator Mundi did not come from the imagination of Leonardo da Vinci. In fact, the Salvator Mundi is an old, Christian iconography with a rich, historical tradition. There are easy to see guidelines that need to be followed for a proper Salvator Mundi. Examples of this being a blessing right hand while the left hand holds an orb. I have noticed, however, that the clothing and hair color can vary. But you do need the hands in their proper

---

1. Davis-Marks, "Newly Discovered Drawing," lines 2–4.

placement. It goes almost without saying that the person depicted needs to be Jesus Christ. And usually, but not every time, Jesus is depicted as being straight on, facing the viewer. This makes it all the more interesting as to why the *Salvator Mundi* was attributed to da Vinci. Yes, he painted prominent religious figures such as John the Baptist, but he was not known to have painted distinct themes that were done by many other artists. Even if Leonardo were to have painted a Salvator Mundi, he would have made it in a way that resembles the rest of his work.

Much of Christian iconography has its roots in the Medieval period. Many of these figures appear flat, giving a straightforward explanation as to what the particular message is. Some early Christians favored *aniconism*, which is the disapproval of the use of images for religious purposes. However, this stance by the early Christians did not last long, as we can now see that a tradition of iconography has prevailed. Two religious figures that were regularly depicted was Mother Mary and Jesus Christ. When the two of them were shown together it was common to see Mary holding the baby with some form of religious semblance being present, such as a halo. Another example of Mother Mary with a young Jesus was the depiction using a *Hodegetria*. This is when she is pointing towards Christ to signify him as the only path towards salvation. Christ then holds his own hand up in a blessing fashion. Seeing the progression of Christian iconography from depicting a *Hodegetria*, and then coming up with a Salvator Mundi, follows the historical thread of displaying Christ as the son of God.

Leonardo was a religious man and painted many religious figures. It is hard though to imagine that he would take on such unoriginal, and even boring subject matter of a Salvator Mundi. The Salvator Mundi iconography is awkward. The lone Christ figure, dressed in colorful robes, holding an orb gives off the impression that you are looking at a mystical wizard, rather than a Messiah. Nothing from the image is described in the Christian Bible. In the gospels, Jesus is forcefully wrapped in purple clothing to sarcastically mock him as being royal. The Salvator Mundi's typically dress him in blue and/or red clothing. An orb is nowhere to be found in the New Testament either, much less Jesus walking around with one in his hand. But the orb can be meant to represent the world, and Jesus is the one holding it. A Salvator Mundi has inherent flaws in its iconography. Despite the cumbersome nature of a Salvator Mundi, at the time it could be held as a strong devotional image. And it works even better for students to practice with, and for artists who have run out of original ideas. This image incorporates all that would be needed for a student, like the painting of human hair, hands at different positions, and robes for the clothing. Essentially the only thing that is absent for a student to use as practice would be painting the feet.

Gerard David, a Netherlandish artist, painted a Salvator Mundi around the same time the other *Salvator Mundi* was painted, and there are stark differences. The similarities between the two, however, is that David also painted lifeless hair on his Salvator Mundi, and a flat face. When comparing the two, it can be tempting to want to attribute the *Salvator Mundi* to da Vinci himself simply because it is a better painting. I would want the focus to be shifted more on the background of the painting instead. Da Vinci's *Salvator Mundi* uses *Chiaroscuro*, an all-black background, and Gerard David uses a similar Chiaroscuro technique for his background as well. The only difference is that David adds a halo surrounding Christ's head. This is not to say that David and da Vinci collaborated. But it does highlight the fact that black backgrounds are a technique that was not unique to Leonardo. David's Salvator Mundi follows the protocols required for this type of iconography and does not deviate. There is little imagination in Gerard David's Salvator Mundi, but when you compare it to the one that is attributed to da Vinci, you can see that there is minimal imagination in that one as well.

The notion of using Salvator Mundi as a theme for Christian iconography even stretches to artists such as Albrecht Dürer and Jan van Eyck in Europe, who made versions of it. As with the art back then, there were many rules that needed to be followed. Contemporary views of art where freedom is a virtue was not practiced throughout most of art history. And regarding a painting such as this, there needs to be a depiction of Christ in robes, with a right blessing hand, and the left hand holding an orb. There are many variations on this, however, every painting we have of the Salvator Mundi at the very least depicts those things. With this being said, an artist that has a decent sense of imagination would be able to skillfully depict this form of iconography in a unique manner. Just because there are rules in place does not mean that variations within those own set of rules cannot be allowed. Several versions of the Salvator Mundi show a glass orb, with a cross fixed to the top of it, this is known as the *Globus Cruciger*. This image has been used since the Middle Ages and was incorporated in other areas of life in addition to paintings, such as being found on currency. The *Salvator Mundi* in question does not have a cross on the top of the orb, as there are several other versions that do not have one either. But it is essential to understand the style of this painting, and the reasons as to why one would see other Salvator Mundi's with a Christian cross on top of the orb.

The *Salvator Mundi* was created during the Renaissance, which was a time of not only great advancements in society, but also a rediscovery of the past. The *Globus Cruciger* harkens back to the times of antiquity where the imagery of someone holding a globe alluded to them holding the world in their hands. There are even depictions of people standing on top of an orb, which would show their dominion over it. One of many examples would be 4th century coins that depict Emperor Constantine I holding an orb. In the 5th century, as Christianity was rising in power, this globe started to be depicted with a cross on top. I view this as a relatively easy way to take imagery that had already existed and add a religious-specific connotation to it. The recycling of known images. It would not take long for royalty to incorporate it for themselves to show the unison between them and God. It also found its way to the Vatican. One of the most prominent locations of a *Globus Cruciger* would be on the Papal Tiara itself. It was worn by Catholic Popes from the 8th century to the early 1960's, in which it was last worn by Pope Paul VI.

This imagery is ancient, but yet there have been little modifications to it over the years. Afterall, an orb with a cross on top of it can really only be depicted in so many ways. What can change, however, is the depiction of Jesus while holding it. We see many similarities with this iconography. But even so, there are many unique aspects to them in their own right. The *Salvator Mundi* that is attributed to Leonardo da Vinci is a standard image. There is nothing that is special about it and looks to only provide a straightforward understanding of what a Salvator Mundi is supposed to be. There is Jesus with long, brown hair, wearing robes, and holding an orb. While Leonardo certainly painted religious figures, he did not paint ancient, religious themes. Each work that he painted was his own, unique creation. Leonardo da Vinci followed the rules at the time for Renaissance paintings, but every work showed his own voice. This *Salvator Mundi* is one of indifference, a painting done by someone who is still learning the craft.

There is also something particularly strange regarding the clothing choice that was depicted in the *Salvator Mundi*. In October 2022, at an art conference in Germany, da Vinci scholar, Philipp Zitzlsperger, shared intriguing research regarding clothing depicted in Christian iconography. He stated that Christ in the *Salvator Mundi* is wearing a blue tunic, which is an odd choice considering other Salvator Mundi's tunics are depicted in red. The collar in this painting is also shown with an intricate golden embroidery. However, no other Salvator Mundi paintings, or any other depictions of Christ during this time, have this type of collar. What Zitzlsperger did discover is that the same low-cut collar with golden embroidery was used on paintings of female saints. Raphael even used this in his portrait of Elisabetta Gonzaga, painted between 1504–1505. Whoever it was that painted the *Salvator Mundi* decided to depict Jesus Christ in women's clothes.[2]

2. Cole, "Role of Leonardo's Workshop," lines 23–25.

Chapter 6: A Curious Man

The Renaissance is the period in which Europe moved out of the Middle Ages and towards modernity which lasted through the 15th and 16th centuries. This great period was coming off of a history of various political and religious upheavals, plagues, and famine. Beginning in Florence, people looked back on the earlier advancements of antiquity, while also forging a new path. The High Renaissance was a short-lived time that lasted from approximately 1495 to 1527, following the sack of Rome by Charles V, Holy Roman Emperor. Great artistic advancements were made during this time due to better understandings of perspective and visual depth. Michelangelo's sculptures *Pietà* and *David* evoke strong emotions while highlighting artistic achievements. Raphael's painting, *La Fornarina*, is another example of not only depicting the human form in a revolutionary manner, but also in pushing the boundaries of how the body is to be viewed. The level of talent coming out of Florence was staggering. Another artist that made the Renaissance so powerful was Leonardo da Vinci.

Leonardo da Vinci was one of the most impressive men to ever live. Adding a parade of praiseworthy synonyms still would not be able to skim the surface of this person's accomplishments. He worked methodically, but quick enough to have accomplished all that he did. When all is said and done, it looks like Leonardo's biggest competitor was himself. He most definitely felt the pressure of competing artists, like Michelangelo. But looking at the state of his existence there was truly no one else who matched his stamina and insight. In fact, it is remarkable to know that Leonardo even bothered with his intense resentment towards Michelangelo due to da Vinci being held in such high regards publicly. His fierce nature towards other genius artists, however, shows a competitive side to his nature. One that wrestles with his own skills and abilities and puts them to the test against other top-level artists. It should also come as no surprise that he also drew up and invented many weapons of war.

There are no records about Leonardo that describe him as a brash, mean person. In fact, everything we know about the man seems to show the opposite. He was born out of wedlock in the town of Vinci and had humble beginnings. Being an illegitimate child got him out of having to do the same profession of his father, who was a notary. This could have had a butterfly effect as if he were to have been forced into the notary trade, he easily could have forgone the arts and sciences. He probably struggled with a form of Attention Deficit Hyperactive Disorder due to his many notes and incomplete projects. Keeping records as required of a notary would not have been a successful venture for Leonardo. Since he was an illegitimate child, he was not allowed to receive a formal education either. This led a young Leonardo to explore how the world worked around him and to focus on the things that could be, rather than being content with the things that already were.

Like all children, he loved to put rocks in streams and watch the water split around them. Swirls of water would be some of Leonardo's earliest known sketches and fascinated him for the rest of his life.[1] The hair in his paintings represent those mesmerizing swirls of water, like in the painting *Saint John the Baptist*. This concept of the movement of water is a regular motif to the appearance of the movement of hair in his paintings. Da Vinci would present himself with questions for his entire life. While he genuinely wanted to know the answers, what seems even more extraordinary are the questions he comes up with. Some of these questions were about what the tongue of a woodpecker looked like. Or if bird's wings moved faster when they flapped upward or downward. Leonardo da Vinci was a man of intense curiosity. And he was

1. Politics and Prose, "Walter Isaacson," 5:51.

able to use his sense of wonder to create his own conditions that allowed for his brilliance to flourish.

At the age of twelve, Leonardo moved to the vibrant city of Florence.[2] Constantinople had recently fallen, which led to an influx of people migrating to this city, greatly increasing its population. The print shop from Guttenberg was founded and publishing became rampant there. This was an eccentric, cosmopolitan city, and someone like da Vinci was able to fit well into an environment such as this. Literacy was at a relatively high rate. There was an abundance of woodcarvers. And while homosexuality was a serious criminal offense, it was rarely prosecuted. Leonardo wore flamboyant clothing, particularly pink and purple tunics that were cut short at the legs. He was left-handed. He was gay. He was a vegetarian. He was an embodiment of what Florence was.[3] The people of Bavaria during this period referred to the citizens of Florence as *Florenzers*, a slang term for homosexuality due to the city's well-known tolerance of it.

We do not know much about his personal life. While we can piece together various records and notes, his day-to-day life left many gaps. He was much more interested in writing his notes on inventions and science than he was about keeping a daily journal. One area of his life that we are confident about is his sexuality. When he was twenty-four years old, he was arrested along with three other men, on charges of sodomy with a male prostitute. These charges were quickly dropped due to one of the men being in close relation to the Medici family.[4] After reviewing the drawings by da Vinci, I think he also preferred to draw nude men over women. When compared to heterosexual male artists who drew more women to men in the nude, it does add to the evidence that he was gay. In addition to the nude drawings, there are also many parody drawings of his paintings that are homoerotic in nature. An example of this is the drawing *Angel Incarnato*, which is a version of his painting *Saint John the Baptist*. A stark difference is

2. Isaacson, *Leonardo da Vinci*, 23.

3. Politics and Prose, "Walter Isaacson," 7:48.

4. Pierpont, "Secret Lives," line 1.

that the drawing includes an exposed, erect penis. The fact that Leonardo never married or produced any known children further adds to the fact of his sexuality.

The Medici family began their rise to prominence in the first half of the 15th century by Cosimo de' Medici in the Republic of Florence. This family created an incredibly successful bank, called the Medici Bank, and they were able to use their financial influence to gain power over Florence. The Medici family used their prestige to have family members become Dukes and Popes, as well as being involved in other various high-ranking roles. They would not only have family members who went on to become Popes and Dukes, but they also had women become Queens of France, Catherine de' Medici, and Marie de' Medici. One area of focus for the Medici family was the arts. Commissions were a regular occurrence for the family as I think that they knew that a city with great art represents a city that is flourishing.

Leonardo's creativity had been with him from an early age. He took part in various theatrical plays that were put on by the Medici family.[5] Every night various performances and debates were produced for both intellectual and entertainment purposes. Today's society looks towards streaming services and podcasts, and the people of Florence at the time would view these productions as their source of a leisurely hobby. Da Vinci oversaw the costumes for many of these pageants.[6] The famous ariel screw drawing from his notebooks, is viewed by most as the first invention of the helicopter. It was actually used as a machine to help bring down flying angels for one of these shows.[7] What is truly remarkable about this is that not only did Leonardo daydream about the possibility of human flight, but that he could set out in ways to make it a reality. And in the case of this early helicopter, he was able to see it come to fruition on the stage. Limitations was not something that seemed to have been of concern to this man.

5. Politics and Prose, "Walter Isaacson," 10:25.
6. Politics and Prose, "Walter Isaacson," 10:33.
7. Worrall, "Genius," line 13.

Even someone who had one of the greatest minds to ever exist still had teachers. At a young age, da Vinci entered the workshop of the famed artist and craftsman Andrea del Verrocchio. Andrea's father, Michele di Francesco Cioni, started out as a brick layer and then became a tax collector. An impressive climb for an individual. Just like how Leonardo's father was a notary, yet he would become a great thinker and artist, Verrocchio had a similar path. It's difficult to know if this is a bond that da Vinci and Verrocchio openly shared. However, it is such a similarity between the two of them that it is hard to ignore the influence. In fact, there would be another glaring similarity between these men. Both would never marry. While there is an overwhelming amount of evidence that Leonardo was gay, there is little information to go off of regarding Verrocchio's own sexuality. Nevertheless, Verrocchio proved to be both an incredible artist and teacher. The poet, Ugolino Verino, referenced Verrocchio in his poems by writing that all decent painters were influenced by him.

Collaboration with artworks is a historical venture. In da Vinci's early twenties, he had the honor of working with Verrocchio on the painting, *The Baptism of Christ*. He was allowed to paint the angel on the end of the painting. This angel has a gorgeous twist of the shoulders and looks adoringly as Jesus while he is being baptized. Verrocchio, in an almost humorous manner, painted the angel next to him with their eyes rolling. I believe this is to suggest that Verrocchio's angel could never be on the same par as the one that Leonardo had made. Another area of this painting that Leonardo da Vinci was able to do was the ripples of water at Christ's feet. Not only was the movement of water painted in a scientifically correct way, but it also alludes to his lifelong obsession with it and its relation to its environment. Leonardo's love for water, and the way it moves, is something that he would play with as a young boy. It was also one of his last sketches before passing away.

It is not just Leonardo's obsession with water and how it relates to the human body that would keep his mind occupied, but rather nature that connects us. He wrote in his notebooks how trees branch out, and that this bears a heavy relation to how human arteries branch out. Da Vinci was quick to point out that these patterns are reflected in every aspect of being. The polymath also spent his time trying to square a circle.[8] In other words, to create a square that has the same area as a circle. This very old geometric challenge is impossible, and it is hard to know if da Vinci knew this. Nevertheless, he would pursuit this as though it would contain the answers to the mysteries of existence. There are many worthless conspiracy theories about Leonardo, such as him placing secret codes within his paintings. However, the actual knowledge that we have of the man is enough for several lifetimes worth of study. Someone who found the relation of swirls of water to the curls of hair. And a person who focused on the similarities of tree branches to the branches of arteries, shows just how deep his thoughts really were. There is no need to add myths to someone of this intellectual stature.

Around the age of thirty he was sent by the Medici family as part of a delegation of creatives to Milan.[9] Out of the many things that the Medici family was known for, their military strength was not one of them. In addition to their skills with banking, they relied heavily on building relationships with the other powers from close by regions. Sharing culture was the best diplomacy. And sending a group of creative people would help strengthen bonds between their neighbors and be seen as a sign of both peace and collaboration. This is a much better strategy than allowing paranoid thoughts of war to enter the discourse. Except da Vinci was not sent to Milan as a scientist or artist. He was sent there as a musician because he was creating beautifully crafted instruments. He sent in an application to the Duke of Milan that was about eleven paragraphs long. Throughout his entire application he stressed his military weapons ingenuity and his overall skills at engineering. It was not until the last paragraph that he mentions that he also knows how to paint.[10] Leonardo da Vinci viewed himself as

8. Politics and Prose, "Walter Isaacson," 19:28.

9. Politics and Prose, "Walter Isaacson," 21:53.

10. Politics and Prose, "Walter Isaacson," 22:39.

someone who created many things, and painting was simply just another method of creation.

Leonardo da Vinci was a fan of collaboration. The notion of the sole artist working alone in their studio was not really much of a conception until about the late 1800s, especially with artists like Vincent van Gogh. In fact, collaborating in the arts has always been a strong method of learning and discovery for people across creative fields. An example of this would be the Milan Cathedral which Leonardo assisted in its design. In addition to being a scientist, artist, and weapons inventor, he was also an architect. Under orders from the Duke of Milan, da Vinci designed the Tiburio, which is a tall tower at the top of the cathedral. This is known to be his first architectural achievement, which is quite remarkable given the nature and size of the project. Collaboration was essential for da Vinci as he only designed that one part of the building, and other architects took on the rest.[11] Each of these collaborators would have to be of the same understanding for its layout in order for it to all successfully come together.

One of his closest friends was the artist and architect, Donato Bramante. In fact, Bramante would make a painting of them together titled and depicted as, *Heraclitus and Democritus*.[12] The painting shows Leonardo with his long and curly hair, short and colorful tunics, and muscular build with a square jawline. It even shows his unique writing style which is written from right to left due to him being left-handed. Both Bramante and da Vinci worked together on various architectural designs and were influenced by the ancient Roman architect and engineer, Vitruvius. This ancient Roman presented the case that all architecture, particularly religious ones, should be simplistic in nature and reflect the human body. Bramante and da Vinci's love for Vitruvius' works brought them into heavy research on his writings of the human body. Leonardo's reading of Vitruvius ultimately led to the drawing of the *Vitruvian Man.* This famous drawing shows Leonardo's desire throughout his life to find a way to somehow square the circle.

11. Isaacson, *Leonardo da Vinci*, 140.
12. Isaacson, *Leonardo da Vinci*, 142.

What is also noticeable about the image is that when you compare it to Bramante's painting of him and da Vinci, you see that it is a self-portrait. The *Vitruvian Man* is a drawing that Leonardo da Vinci did of himself.[13]

The *Vitruvian Man* is both a scientific and artistic masterpiece. Then again, da Vinci viewed the sciences and the arts as the same thing. His pursuits led him to creations of weapons, instruments, and paintings all through his understanding of engineering. This drawing has perfect proportions which are heavily reflected in his notes on measurements and the human form. His self-portrait also shows him within both the circle and the square, and how the body is in relation to each of them. If the square cannot be in full participation of the circle, at least the human body can be. This incredible mathematical precision is simply incomparable to the *Salvator Mundi* painting. The *Salvator Mundi* has an awkward appearance that is full of inaccurate proportions, but the *Vitruvian Man* has a strong balance to it that is reflected at every line and curve. The drawing is intentional, and each aspect is well thought out. The *Salvator Mundi* looks as if someone is still learning to draw.

In his forties, he painted *The Last Supper*. This mural is theatrical in nature and alludes back to his time working as a young boy in the theatre. There are colorful robes, dramatic movements of the figures, and they are all facing the viewer. It appears Leonardo used his history with the theatre to engage the viewers like a stage would. If you look at the walls that he painted on in *The Last Supper*, you can see that the left side is darker than the one on the right. This is not due to a mistake of Leonardo's, and it is also not due to aging. In fact, it was intentional. In the room where the mural exists you see that there are windows on the left-hand side, where the natural sunlight comes in. Leonardo intentionally made the wall on the right side of *The Last Supper* lighter because that is where the actual sunshine rests in the room. Everything Leonardo painted was intentional.[14] He made it a point to not make mistakes.

13. Politics and Prose, "Walter Isaacson," 31:34.
14. Kemp, *Living with Leonardo*, 34.

Later in life, Leonardo da Vinci continued with his various pursuits. This included his love of flight and his desire to have humans be up in the skies with the birds. In his notebooks we find many drawings of different contraptions that often mimic a resemblance of birds. Accompanied by these drawings are many lines of notes. One of these notes mentions that if he himself did not create a successful mode for humans to fly, then he is certain someone else in the future would invent it. In addition to attempted creations for flight, he had other ideas such parachutes, robotic-like soldiers, catapults for wartime, and many other original ideas. With the blend of having been a perfectionist, as well as having a scattered mind, da Vinci moved gracefully from one project to the next. This method of inventing allowed him to come up with many wonderful ideas but did not allow him to perfect the functions for most of them. Despite the many notebooks we have of da Vinci, there is still not a single mention, or drawing, that links to the *Salvator Mundi*.

Approaching older age, da Vinci would spend the years of 1513–1516 at the Apostolic Palace in Rome at the request of the Medici family.[15] Lorenzo de' Medici's son, Giovanni, was now Pope and assumed the name, Leo X. He was a major patron of the arts. During this time, it is believed that Leonardo had a stroke, and this led to several more. These illnesses debilitated him and prevented him from painting consistently. In 1515, Francis I of France recaptured Milan, and the following year, Leonardo entered the French King's service. He lived in a château known as Clos Lucé, which was close to the King's own personal residence. Despite his illnesses, Leonardo worked continuously, and the King made regular visits to see his progress. Some of the projects that he took on for the King involved designing a castle town. Also, he drew up designs for a mechanical lion that could not only move but would reveal a collection of flower lilies when tapped with a wand.[16]

At the end of his life, having survived several strokes, Leonardo da Vinci is still working. Even with being unable to do much

15. Ottino, *Paintings of Leonardo*, 86.
16. Wallace, *World of Leonardo*, 163–4.

painting, his mind continued with its curious nature. Thinking about existence and his place in the world was not something that he could just turn off. He was not obsessed with working, rather his work was who he was. He thought about nature and wondered why things were the way that they were. While some of his inventions were successful, many would not actually work too well if created. It seems as if the point of creating was to see if he could push beyond the boundaries that were already established. On the very last page of his notebooks, we see that he was still attempting to square the circle. He drew various right triangles of different sizes and wrote descriptions on how he could further go about it. At his last moments he was still pursuing his goals. It is at the last line at the bottom of this page that he would write, "But, the soup is getting cold." Leonardo da Vinci would shortly thereafter die with King Francis I by his side.[17]

17. Politics and Prose, "Walter Isaacson," 47:02.

Chapter 7: Shaky Evidence

The *Salvator Mundi* could not achieve its attribution to Leonardo da Vinci simply because one or two people wished it. There are many moving parts that need to go along for that to happen, and it needs to be systematic. I do not claim to know the motivations of the people involved in its attribution, and I am sure that some of them truly believe the painting to have been done by Leonardo. Simultaneously, I am sure that others involved do not actually think that Leonardo made the painting. I do also believe some people who have attributed it to da Vinci do not really have a strong stance on whether he painted it or not. Speculation can be a dirty game, and I do not intend to get muddy. Top Leonardo da Vinci scholars are not in unison on who painted it either, and I expect this controversy to not go away anytime soon, if ever. What I do see are simply opinions from some experts who believe that da Vinci painted this. But, if it is their opinions that are carrying the weight, then why are the opinions of other prominent da Vinci scholars being diminished? There are some basic points from some specialists as to why they claim that Leonardo is the man behind the artwork.

Waldemar Januszczak, an art critic, claims the *Salvator Mundi* to have been by da Vinci because it is a creepier version than other depictions of Christ at the time. He also acknowledges that the *Salvator Mundi* is not like any other painting by Leonardo.[1] A fairly weak reason to ascribe this painting to da Vinci. A more

[handwritten marginal note: Seems like pretty deep in the mud.]

1. Januszczak, "Miracle of da Vinci," line 1.

37

serious claim is that in the year 1650, Wenceslaus Hollar created an etching of a Salvator Mundi that only somewhat resembles the painting in question. And at the bottom of the etching, it is written in Latin that it is after the original artwork by Leonardo da Vinci. This is used as a substantial piece of evidence as it directly calls out the existence of this iconography by da Vinci. This is not enough to persuade me in either direction, and I am more inclined to dismiss this for two reasons provided in the rhetorical:

How would Hollar even know the painting was truly done by Leonardo?

Why would a nearly 150-year gap between the creation of the *Salvator Mundi* painting versus the Hollar etching be considered substantial evidence?

A decent piece of evidence that da Vinci made the work is that there appears to be a handprint pressed above Jesus' left eyebrow. Leonardo was left-handed and was known to put the heal of his right hand into the work to obtain a more soft, tonal transition. Scholars that claim Leonardo is the person behind the painting do not state that this evidence alone is enough to say he's the one who created it. However, it is an interesting bit of information that they can incorporate as evidence. This handprint could also have been from one of Leonardo's students. I do not view it as too much of a stretch to say that a devoted student of his would try out some of the unorthodox techniques his teacher used. And I also think it is acceptable to say that the handprint is in fact that of da Vinci. This is because it does not mean that he painted the *Salvator Mundi*. It could simply be a teacher showing a pupil a method that he uses in his own artworks. Workshops in the time of the Renaissance were collaborative in nature.[2]

The *Salvator Mundi* underwent several infrared X-rays to see parts of the painting that would be unknown to the human eye.[3] These examinations showed other pentimenti had taken place, particularly above Christ's garment. Another aspect that the X-ray picked up was the priming that was utilized for the artwork. Da

2. Culotta, "Workshop in Italian Renaissance," lines 1–2.
3. Modestini, "Materials & Techniques," line 33.

Vinci was known to tint various parts of the priming before he began his work, and with the *Salvator Mundi*, the infrared X-rays picked up priming that appears to have bits of glass blended up into it.[4] This type of priming is rather eccentric, and yet it still does not directly point to the work having been done by Leonardo. However, priming a painting is usually seen as a much less important factor on the creation of the work. A student using broken glass in their priming would be making a daring decision for someone who is still learning, but it is possible. The findings of broken glass in the original layers of the priming are still a fascinating discovery that could help tip the evidence towards a da Vinci attribution. However, it is not nearly enough to use this as a main source of evidence, and this was not a technique that he did with his other works.

Some people who fully, and partially attribute this painting to Leonardo da Vinci, can claim that the right blessing hand was certainly done by Leonardo. I have heard them make two main arguments as to why they believe this. The first point they will make is the pentimento of the thumb. They see that the artist originally had the thumb in one position, and then changed his mind and moved it to another. Of course, even students would utilize a pentimento because mistakes and changes of the mind is something that happens with us humans. The second point that they make is that the hand looks very modern, and much in the style of Leonardo. I tend to agree. This painting is a total trainwreck, even after it was stripped down to its original layers of paint. The work is just not good. However, the right hand is easily the best part of the painting. It was clearly crafted with care and took skill to produce. People can claim that da Vinci painted this right hand, and nothing else. Even if this were true, it would not be enough to attribute the *Salvator Mundi* to him directly. Instead, it would be attributed as something along the lines of saying that it was painted in Leonardo's Workshop, with possible help from Leonardo on the right hand. But again, that is only if it was proven to have been painted by him. My argument against the authorship of the right hand

4. Modestini, "Materials & Technique," line 39.

to Leonardo is that many of his students, and many other artists at the time, were fully capable of painting a hand in this fashion. Leonardo was not the only one with this capability.

What is pointed out by art experts about the *Salvator Mundi* is the orb that he is holding in his left hand. This is a standard part of any Salvator Mundi iconography, even though the type of orb can vary by depicting it as being crafted by different material, like being of glass or bronze. Some art scholars who attribute this painting to Leonardo say that this orb was painted to be shown as rock crystal. They can argue that the orb shows various markings and faults within it that would suggest this. The reason why this is used as a bit of evidence for their side is because of Leonardo's fascination with geology, and that he would have understood how to properly depict a clear rock crystal.[5] They can further argue that this was his own way of pushing the boundaries of presenting Jesus in this manner. And then they can take it even further by pointing out the three dots in the orb to represent the stars in the sky, suggesting that Jesus is the Savior for all of existence. Of course, many leaps of faith are taken about this orb. The initial claim that this orb is of rock crystal is merely an educated thought without evidence. Therefore, everything that builds from this is coming off a shaky foundation. Nevertheless, a painting of an orb made of rock crystal still does not prove that it was painted by Leonardo da Vinci.

Looking through the thousands of pages in Leonardo da Vinci's notebooks, there appears two sketches that can be suggested as preparatory drawings for a Salvator Mundi. They display a person's right arm covered with a robe, and the centerpiece of the robe covering the chest. These two drawings are held in the Royal Collection and regularly referenced as evidence. However, these drawings are nothing like the painting of the *Salvator Mundi*. In fact, they do not match at all. These art scholars who attribute the authorship to Leonardo will also make dubious claims that the *Salvator Mundi* has a certain type of presence about it, or that it provides a religious experience. This is not evidence. It does provide a way for the scholars to say that they can simply tell that it

5. Gresham College, "Martin Kemp," 31:52.

is a Leonardo just by looking at it. Yes, they see the locks of hair, a crystal orb, and an intricately painted blessing hand. But they also add in that they can feel its presence in addition to whatever else they deem to be evidence. This sort of claim also does not account for the many other art scholars who do not feel anything powerful from the *Salvator Mundi* when viewing it. I know that I feel nothing but indifference when looking at it. There are several claims as to why some think that Leonardo painted this work, but there is no smoking gun. The minimal evidence they provide is not enough to equate attribution.

Chapter 8: The Before Time

As long as I can remember I have always felt a need to create. This almost instinctual feeling inside of myself feels like it is less of a choice and much more of a compulsion. A thought that regularly comes to me is the notion of free will. We all want to be the ones who are in charge and make the decisions over our own lives, and maybe this can be somewhat true. But what is also true is that we cannot choose the time period in which we are born into. We cannot choose who our parents are, or the economic class we are raised in. We cannot control the things that happen to us, and we cannot even control the things that don't happen to us. A typical response to say is that we control how we want to react to certain moments. Even then, how we respond to situations is based on things that we have already gone through and can comprehend. I wonder what would have happened to someone like Albert Einstein had he been born in, say, the 1600s. Maybe he would have contributed something to the sciences back then, but it is probably safe to say that it would not have been the Theory of Relativity. Or what if Leonardo da Vinci was born in 1950s America? I think that he would have contributed to the arts, but it most likely would have looked much different than the art he actually made.

I cannot help but think this about myself as well too. What if I was blind? I would still be an artist, but my artwork would be much different. And the notion of being a Copyist at the Louvre probably would never happen. As both a child, and as an adult, I took piano lessons. But as much as I practiced, I was never where I was truly supposed to be at with the instrument. Another person's talent at the piano would easily soar over my own abilities, even if the two of us had the same resources and put in the same amount of practice. In my early twenties, I gave a brief shot at acting, and honestly speaking, I was terrible at it. Though I did get some credits in local short films and had a supernumerary (non-singing) role with the Portland Opera, my skillset to transform into someone else was never decent. But what if I caught a random, lucky break and managed to somehow get regular, professional acting roles? It is safe to say that I would still be a terrible actor, but my focus would be on acting. Sure, I may still make paintings and sculptures, but my attention would have to be placed more towards the craft of acting. This all brings up more questions than actual answers, but it is the questions that help guide us. Questioning topics such as this shows that everything in all of existence builds from the past. Whatever I have created before, will lead me to where I am at in the present moment.

My innate feeling to be creative has always been with me and has never left. My father instilled in me at a very young age that you never want to be mediocre. Being average was one of the worst things a human could be. That stuck with me. The realization that we have this one life to live makes for an interesting pressure to be placed on yourself. You don't want to live a life that is based on some human-crafted algorithm, you want to do something that sets yourself apart. Something that you can be proud of. I find much beauty in the regular, day to day life. However, we all experience that, and we can choose to look at life in a positive or negative light. What I have always been driven towards is finding a way to separate myself from the norm. I found the remedy to that by being an artist at the age of twenty-four. My initial goal of being an artist was to simply sell one piece of art that I made. But I would sell that piece of art to a collector in Manhattan almost immediately after creating it. The goal I had set for myself seemed nearly impossible, especially since we always hear about artists struggling to sell their work. I then had to raise the stakes for myself, and that would be to sign with a legitimate art gallery.

There are two types of art galleries; the real ones, and the fake ones. These fake art galleries are essentially just a *pay for play* business model. What they do is charge artists an application fee, then require monthly dues, while also demanding that the artist works a shift there for free every month. On top of this, the gallery often takes 50% of whatever art piece is sold. In other words, if the artist's monthly dues are $200, and they sell one painting a month for $400, the gallery takes half, and then the artist only breaks even for that month. Not to mention that the artist is required to devote an entire day of working for free at the gallery. So really the artist is now operating at a loss. If any artists are currently reading this, let this be an example of the type of gallery to never do business with, regardless of how they present their business model to you. It is a scam. The other type of gallery is the legitimate one where the artist is solely responsible for creating the art and handing it over to the curator. From there, the legitimate gallery puts on group and solo shows. For clarity, when I say *gallery*, it is only in reference to the legitimate ones.

The galleries themselves are put into three categories: Small-level, Mid-level, and Mega. The Small-level galleries sign unknown artists and bring them in for one art show at a time. These smaller ones sell art that is affordable to the average person and is a great way for artists to hopefully transition to Mid-level galleries. Mid-level galleries host a wide range of artists, many of which are relatively well-known, and the price points tend to be much higher. Then there are the Mega galleries, and they are essentially for the most famous and expensive artists. Gagosian and David Zwirner are among these big-name players, which have multiple locations and high-profile clients. All of this operates as a necessary ecosystem. Without the smaller and mid-range galleries, then the Mega galleries would not have artists who could move up to them. Each level of these galleries acts as a form of test to see how well an artist's work can sell. Artists must develop their craft over time to hone their skills and obtain a loyal collector base. Each level of the gallery system works in unison and filters out the less talented, and less dedicated artists.

Chapter 8: The Before Time

To be taken seriously as an artist, people need to believe that you're an actual artist instead of just a hobbyist. If someone is to be an artist then their time needs to be involved in the arts, including regular gallery and museum visits. Like how if someone wants to be a writer, then they must also be a reader. I learn a lot from my time spent going to art exhibits, such as deciphering the differences between good art and bad art, and I try to incorporate those lessons into my own work. Not too long after selling my first artwork I would end up signing with a professional art gallery. And over the next several years I was fortunate enough to sign with two more Small-level galleries. Every accomplishment I have had with art has led me to want to achieve something more. While I have always been satisfied and proud of what I do, there is a constant feeling inside of me that wants to do more. I feel like there is always a new goal to go after, a new target. In a weird sense, it feels like no matter what I do in the arts it will never be enough for me. I think this is just my own way of staying motivated and not stagnate.

My artwork does not have just one style to it. To be honest, I become easily bored if I am just painting the same way for every work. I like to change subject matter and alter perception with what I am creating, such as using various media. When creating art, the shared trait with all my work is to try and take the viewer out of their current emotional state. If I can get the person who is looking at the artwork to feel an inner emotion, something other than their baseline feelings, then at least I have achieved something with them. Indifference to a work of art is much worse than a dislike for a particular piece. In fact, I think indifference to anything is the purest form of dissatisfaction. Something being so unworthwhile that it does not even garner a reaction from someone. That is the worst thing an artist can do is make something of utter indifference. Art has been with humans since the beginning, and it has changed drastically from the cave paintings up to this present moment. I try to learn as much as I can from all of it and see how it relates to my own self as an artist. Creating art feels like more of a need for me to do rather than something that feels like an option.

At twenty-seven, several years after signing with my first gallery, my own artwork ended up in an art museum. I had been on the hunt to get an artwork of mine, even if temporarily, into one. A bold move, but I felt that I needed to go after something bigger than just doing a few shows at an art gallery a year. After discussing with a department at the Portland Art Museum in Oregon, they agreed to bring a sculpture of mine I had designed specifically for the museum, into their collection. The sculpture itself was a *found object*, which is an artwork that takes pieces that are already made and claiming it as its own sculpture. The early pioneer of this was Marcel Duchamp, who created the artwork, *Fountain*. It was a men's urinal that was turn upside down. Duchamp's artwork was presented in 1917, the same year of the Communist Russian Revolution, and exactly one hundred years before the sale of the *Salvator Mundi*. My sculpture was a small mason jar, with exposed film inside of it that spiraled up to the top of a gold-colored lid. I titled it, *Theory of Film*. In essence, the artwork was meant to suggest the fragile nature of existence, the fragile protecting the fragile. It was also a way to pay homage to the history of cinema, as this sculpture was displayed in the film department wing of the art museum.

Signing with multiple art galleries and getting an artwork of mine into a museum is something that most artists will not achieve. And I do not want to sound ungrateful, because I am certainly beyond ecstatic and overly thankful, but achieving that at only the age of twenty-seven leaves an existential question. *Well, what do I do now?* The next couple of years I continued to show at galleries and sell work, but when I was approaching thirty, my wife asked me what I wanted to accomplish in the next decade. I told her I wanted to get into another museum. Fortunately, I did not have to wait a decade to do this. Right at the age of thirty I got my art into another museum. The New Hampshire Museum of Fine Art accepted another found object art piece of mine for their own collection. This artwork was a piece of poplar wood with a nail partially hammered into the top of it, I titled it, *Towers*. The sculpture is intended to highlight human innovation and building towards a future rather than reverting backwards. I had doubled down with getting my work into museums. Getting my art into a museum was no longer a once in a lifetime venture. These were barriers that I had broken down through sheer determination.

It can be easy to feel that the art world is rigged because in some ways it is. You will always find a gallerist that gives a solo-show to their cousin. Or the artist who signs with a gallery because they are friends with someone else's friend. However, this is much more the exception than it is the norm. Smaller galleries want to represent artists who not only create good work but are also committed to being an artist. Galleries need to pay the bills and pay their staff; they cannot take on hobbyists simply for this reason. And the larger galleries can only take on established artists who already bring in high revenue. There is no secret formula for getting into a gallery other than to produce quality art that the gallery has a desire in displaying and thinks that they can sell. As far as museums go, they only collect art that fits in with their institution, and that was made by an artist whom they deem to be decent enough for a museum. The reason why many people think the art world is rigged is because of the high amount of rejection that occurs. I have been told *No* by many galleries and museums. The art world, regardless of what your position is in it, requires thick skin. If you are an artist, then your job is to make the best art that you can. Everything else will come together after that.

While preparing for my Copyist work in the Louvre, I focused on different areas of *Saint John the Baptist* to gain a true sense of how da Vinci went about the work. I reviewed various drawings and paintings of his as there are many connecting similarities. I also did a ton of practice sketches and practice paintings so I could figure out his techniques in a practical manner. Immediately I came across the challenge of his use of blending, and the different moments of pressure that he applied to certain areas. I investigated this process on the *Salvator Mundi* and there was not the same consistencies I found when making various renditions of it. There is an overall lack of blending, shading, and depth. In all fairness, this is just me going off of my own sketches and recreations of works by da Vinci. Also, the *Salvator Mundi* has been heavily repainted. My practice renditions of the *Salvator Mundi* did not mirror at all the renditions of other paintings by Leonardo, like the *Saint John the Baptist* or the *Lady with an Ermine*. The *Salvator Mundi* was flat out not painted by him.

Chapter 9: Not Dressed for the Occasion

First glance at the *Salvator Mundi* shows a dull image. There is nothing about the work that pulls the viewer in, whether they have a trained eye for art or not. It is awkward and lifeless. *Salvator Mundi* does not have the presence of the Christian Savior that delivers his faithful followers from damnation. Instead, the painting is mopey and lethargic. The hand that holds the orb looks unsure as to why it is there. The blessing hand represents more of a child in a classroom raising their hand to use the restroom than it does of any spiritual power. And worse than that, the face itself looks more like a human rat rather than of an eccentric Jewish preacher claiming to be the Messiah. The painting is lifeless when you stare at it for even a moment. Stare at it even longer, and you will quickly realize that there is no sign at all of a pulse ever returning. The foundations of this painting, meaning its very outline, is deadpan. While the skill level of the *Salvator Mundi* is decent for other artists in general, it is nowhere near the level of what da Vinci was capable of.

He said the hand was well done earlier

A glaring issue with attributing the *Salvator Mundi* to Leonardo da Vinci is that Christ is depicted as being head on. There is no curvature to his body, no tilt of his head, no twist of the hips. Leonardo never painted a single subject straightforward like this one. Look at his other paintings, they all twist. None are as boring as this one either. *Saint John the Baptist*, da Vinci's final painting, even has a dramatic turn at the waste as his right arm curves with a finger pointing upwards. The *Salvator Mundi* is thought to have been painted around 1499–1510. *Saint John the Baptist* was

Reef safe
Sunscreen

painted around 1513–1516. And *The Last Supper* was painted from 1495–1498. This means that people who attribute the *Salvator Mundi* to Leonardo da Vinci are forced to acknowledge that he went from painting *The Last Supper*, to then make the subpar *Salvator Mundi*, and then make the mind-blowing *Saint John the Baptist*. Even with *The Last Supper*, none of the 13 individuals depicted on it have a lifeless, straightforwardness about them. Jesus Christ in the middle of that work even has his arms spread out with a tilted head. It could be more forgivable if he painted the *Salvator Mundi* in his adolescence while still learning the craft, but certainly not at the height of his career.

On a purely visual scale, we can notice quite a few red flags of this being amateurish work. The jawline is not even on both sides. This automatically gives off a sense of inauthenticity because we can compare other paintings Leonardo did and we do not find this issue in any one of them. The jawlines of his figures are perfect. Imagine if the jaw of the *Ginevra de' Benci* painting, or the *Portrait of a Musician*, which has a particularly strong jawline, were to have been malformed. The works of art would have immediately been laughed at and deemed not worthy of a Renaissance master. Crooked jawlines, particularly in the period in which da Vinci lived, would have been done by a student. Maybe it could be argued that an experienced artist was making the intentional decision for his subject to have the misshaped jaw. It is hard though to fathom a religious artist depicting Jesus in this manner. With all of this being said, artists are not perfect. Many great artists have had trouble painting body parts, notoriously the hands and feet. Jawlines, however, are non-negotiable.

If you think that this painting looks awkward, then that is because it is awkward. And awkwardness is not something that even da Vinci's biggest critics would accuse him of. The only exception to this rule is if they also happen to believe that he painted the *Salvator Mundi*. One of the major reasons for why this painting appears strange is because Christ's nose is depicted like a hockey stick. You are given this *Romanesque*-looking strong nose, and then it weirdly hooks at the end. The curvature of the nose is so abnormal that it looks almost like a deformity. Another reason for the strange appearance is that the eyes are not aligned. His left eye is bigger than the right eye and they are not at much of a balance with one another. Every other painting by Leonardo da Vinci shows a proper balance of body parts. With how much he knew about anatomy, it is hard to fathom that he would slip on something so basic as the size of the eyes.

I have heard people attempt to justify the misshaped and uneven eyes by claiming da Vinci was using what is referred to as the *Christ Pantocrator*. This term is loosely translated to mean *Almighty* and is solely attributed to the depiction of Jesus Christ. The *Christ Pantocrator* was mainly used by Orthodox Eastern Catholics and depicts Jesus with one of his eyes as being larger than the other. It is thought that this style was used to show Christ's dual nature of being both man and God. The oldest depiction that we have of this old style is *The Christ Pantocrator of St. Catherine's Monastery at Sinai*, which was painted in the 6th century. It is unlikely that he would have chosen that style in one of his own works primarily because Leonardo looked to break conventions, not follow them. All of his known paintings, from *Lady with an Ermine* to *Saint John the Baptist*, not only pushed boundaries, but also helped redefine what the painted portrait could be. Using an obscure, ancient method of depicting Jesus does not fit well in his repertoire.

There are several sets of curls of hair on Jesus' head in the painting that I have heard some scholars claim as evidence that Leonardo created this work. An issue that arises from this stance is that the rest of his hair tends to fall flat. Highlighting only a few strands of hair with elegant curls while leaving the rest to be muted and boring is not a stylistic choice of Leonardo. It could, however, be argued that da Vinci painted those curls, while a student painted the rest of the hair. But that seems to create an even more serious question. If da Vinci painted the curls, then wouldn't a student at least attempt to paint their own set of curls on it as well? This is being said, of course, with the assumption that da Vinci even painted the curly haired aspects of the *Salvator Mundi*. Leonardo was not the only person in the workshop that was capable of painting locks of hair. It is just as believable that students combined their own abilities with what they had learned from da Vinci to paint hair that way. Regardless of someone's stance with the hair, there is not the slightest bit of evidence that Leonardo even did as much as flick some paint on them.

The cheeks are also asymmetrical. Just like with the misshapen jawline, this is an error that someone like Leonardo da Vinci just would not have made. It is almost like a yin and yang with regards to the cheeks, as the right one is more sunken, and the left cheek bulges out. This could be more easily excused if the person was depicted as being in motion. However, the *Salvator Mundi* depiction is that of stillness. This lack of congruency furthers the distortion of Christ's face and does not represent what Christians would imagine the Son of God to appear as. The cheekbones themselves even look to be uneven, with the right one being raised higher than the left. A shift such as this would be used if there was a tilt to the head, but the head of this *Salvator Mundi* is depicted as only being upright and positioned forward. Mistakes such as this one could be excused if painted by a student, but there just does not seem to be a reason for such sophomoric mistakes by a well-trained artist.

Sfumato is a technique that seeks to remove the use of lines as a visual. This method is to instead allow for the tones in an artwork to gradually shade into other parts of the picture and create a more realistic image. Leonardo da Vinci spent much of his life being fascinated by how the human eye functions and it is quite impressive considering how much he was able to uncover about it. He learned that the eye does not look at objects as straight on and flat, but instead that there is a curvature about what they see. Our peripherals catch what is beside us and pick up the sides of figures in front of us. This is reflected in all his paintings. From examining his paintings, he clearly makes it a point to depict his figures as being three-dimensional and does this on a two-dimensional surface. While Leonardo was quite talented at executing this process, he was not the only artist at the time who was capable of such a task. Lesser-known artists, like Andrea Solario (1460–1524), was also well-versed in this technique.

Andrea Solario was born in Milan and is a classic example of an Italian Renaissance artist, even though his name and work is not widely known. Solario was a follower of da Vinci, and you can see the influence of style in his works. This is particularly found in his 1506–7 painting, *Salome Receives the Head of St John the Baptist*, where tight locks of curly hair are depicted. The use of the sfumato technique is also evident in his 1513 painting, *Christ Carrying the Cross*. The transition of Jesus' high cheekbones transition with subtle shading down to his jawline. He also depicts a prominent nose that is not drawn out by harsh, straightedge lines. And you can see that the depiction of the lips, mouth, and cheeks are not separated by direct lines either. Instead, they blend at the edges and transition outward to depict a more realistic looking face. So, while da Vinci may have been the master at the sfumato method, he was not the only one capable of achieving this feat.

There are also issues with the clothing and its design. When viewing paintings that da Vinci had done you can see the vibrant intricacies of them. His painting, *Benois Madonna*, carries an intentional use of color which then shades away into different gradients based on the gravitational pull of the fabric. Her right hand is lifted with her palm facing the ceiling and you can see her sleeve begin to slide downward. You can also make out where her knee bends and the pulling of her robe that would occur from this. With the *Salvator Mundi*, we do not see any of this genius insight. The clothing is flat and the design on the harness is rather boring. If anything is impressive at all on the clothing it is the straight lines painted on the design itself. And painting straight lines is something that pupils of a Renaissance workshop would have been assigned to from their teacher. The artist didn't even really bother to do much shadowing work on the robe itself either. They even have Christ's left shoulder raised higher than the right shoulder, and account for no realistic changes to the robe because of this. The clothing itself screams that this was a task assigned to a student to complete.

Selling Leonardo

When scaling outward to view the *Salvator Mundi* as a whole, it is a very claustrophobic painting. Jesus is crammed into the canvas, and it does not allow any grace for a natural figure to form. In fact, it is such a tight-fitting image that you could be forgiven for thinking that the artwork was trimmed on its edges. The same was once thought of the *Mona Lisa* as being trimmed. On either side of the *Mona Lisa* painting, you can see parts of columns that appear cut off at the edge of the canvas. The difference between these two paintings regarding the cutoff imagery is that the *Mona Lisa* has the columns cut off because it helps to add to the landscape encapsulating the woman. The *Mona Lisa* is also not claustrophobic in the slightest and provides a visual depth of proper proportion to the seated woman. This cannot be said of the *Salvator Mundi* because the proportions look to be a flat-out error. It is worth mentioning that neither the *Mona Lisa* nor the *Salvator Mundi* was ever actually trimmed. The imagery that we have is the imagery that was always there. There are no missing parts to either painting.

A glaring issue with this cramped work is the cropped thumb holding the sphere. The tip of the left thumb of the *Salvator Mundi* is nonexistent and shows that the artist did not plan for this. Some people have suggested that later versions of the Salvator Mundi were copies of this one. The problem with this assertion is that really there are only a few similarities with the *Salvator Mundi* in question and the later works. Some faces are rounder than others, some have different pattern designs than others, and some even have different colored clothes. And more importantly, not one of these supposed copies depict a cropped thumb. While these depictions of a Salvator Mundi have minor similarities between one another, they are all different enough that it is quite the leap to suggest that it was painted by Leonardo da Vinci. It is even more egregious to suggest that the painting was used as an example for his students to recreate. Misdiagnosing the proportions of a painting suggests the work of a student, not the work of an artist who runs their own workshop. It must also be said that the left hand was poorly executed, especially when compared to the right hand.

The left hand is smaller and more delicate than the right hand, appearing that it is almost like the hand of a child.

The strength of this *Salvator Mundi* attribution to da Vinci falls in its right hand. Ask any artist what the hardest body part is to paint and if they do not say the foot then they will say the hand. This depiction of the right hand in this painting is technical, and a high level of skill was involved. Its proportions are great, there is a steady movement that radiates from it, and it gives the appearance of being outside of the canvas itself. Regardless of the issue with the pentimento and the thumb on the blessing hand, it is painted remarkably. This hand is painted so well that this does appear to be the driving force as to why some art scholars attribute it to da Vinci. Some people have suggested that even if Leonardo did not lay down a single paint stroke anywhere else on the canvas, he at least painted the right blessing hand. I personally have my doubts. Cesare da Sesto (1477–1523), another talented but obscure follower of Leonardo's, had the ability to paint human hands very well too. This is evident in his painting, *Salome* (1510-20). This is not to suggest that Sesto is the one who painted the blessing hand of the *Salvator Mundi*. But it is to further show that many artists had the same capability, and that Leonardo da Vinci is not the only one who could have painted this hand.

The strongest bit of evidence that would allow me to have a more forgiving perspective of the *Salvator Mundi* is if it was known to be an unfinished painting. Critiquing a work that is not yet completed is an unfair game to play, even if it was done by da Vinci. I am sure that the early stages of the *Mona Lisa* were probably not that great. The issue with this though is that the *Salvator Mundi* is most certainly a finished work. There are no serious scholars, regardless of where they fall on the attribution issue, that think it is unfinished. I agree with them. Sure, maybe the artist behind this painting could claim that they would have preferred to lengthen a couple more curls of hair or add another shadow on the robe. But we know what an unfinished painting by Leonardo da Vinci looks like, such as with *The Adoration of the Magi*. For all practical purposes, it is a safe assumption to say that the *Salvator*

Mundi is in fact a completed painting, and that its artist had no remaining desires to change anything.

A final piece to point out regarding the visuals of the *Salvator Mundi* is the crystal orb, or rather, the appearance of the robe that the viewer can see through the orb. There is no visual distortion. If you took a photograph of yourself holding an orb, there would be an apparent contortion with the view of your clothing behind it. The artist of the *Salvator Mundi* opted to paint that portion of the robe as if there was not a clear globe in front of it. Arguments can be made that da Vinci decided not to make any distortions of the robe through the orb itself, as this would distract the viewer from the overall visuals. There are problems with an assertion such as this one because the artist did not seem to be worried at all regarding any other flaws in the painting. Misshaped jawlines, a crooked nose, and a cropped thumb for just a few examples. This entire painting is a mess. The fact that there is no visual distortion of the robe behind the orb is just one of the many examples that this was created by an amateur.

Chapter 10: Where is the Provenance?

A strong indicator that an artwork was done by a particular artist is the history of where the work has been. An example of this would be a photograph of an artist posing with the painting in their studio. This would provide sufficient evidence as who to attribute that particular painting to. From both a dealer and a collector's perspective, being able to trace the path of a piece of art directly from the artist's possession to its current location is most ideal. Long, unknown gaps of where a work has been can raise significant questions regarding its authorship. With the many talented forgers in the world, it is easier than ever to replicate the style of famous artists. Forgers can take old canvases, use handmade paints, and apply various heating methods to create a visual of aging cracks in the work. It can then be passed off as having been done by an important artist like Cezanne or Picasso. If you have proper provenance, then that significantly minimizes the chance of error or scam with the work. The unfortunate aspect is that some of the world's most important works of art do not have a strong provenance, and that is where the reliance on the trained eye of scholars can come into focus.

Provenance is the history of ownership of a work of art. The best provenance is one that carries a direct line from the artist to where the artwork is currently located. The more gaps in the lineage of the provenance, then the more questions that arise as to who may have created the work. Of course, provenance is not everything, but it is a big part. There are other areas that can be used to help narrow down the possibility of who created it. Some examples of this would be the type of paint and canvas that was used, the artistic style of the work, and how old the art piece is. If those examples are clearly present and if it can be paired with a strong provenance, then it leaves little doubt regarding its attribution. The *Salvator Mundi* does carry some of these qualities, such as it is having been painted on walnut, a favorite of the polymath for use as a canvas. But there are still more factors that need to be considered. A great way to help with this is if the artist did any preliminary drawings of the work in a sketchbook, or if they wrote about it somewhere. There are so many factors at play when a work of art does not have a strong provenance.

An essential area regarding an artwork's provenance is being able to follow who specifically owned it along the way. Often the more prominent the owner of a work, then the higher importance that artwork achieves. If you have a talented artist who makes a great piece of art, and then it is owned by a high-status individual, then that painting is going to automatically be worth a fortune. The painting, *White Center (Yellow, Pink and Lavender on Rose)*, executed by Mark Rothko in 1950, was bought by David Rockefeller in 1960. When Rockefeller put the painting up for auction at Sotheby's in 2007, they were anticipating it to go for around $40 million, but the final price it ended up selling for was over $72 million. The buyers of this Rothko were the Royal Family of Qatar.[1] With the strong provenance of American business royalty and Qatari royalty, if this painting were to go to auction again it would likely acquire an even higher price tag. If you follow major auction house sales for art, it is likely that you will come across a history of ownership for the work that they are selling. Provenance is important to the people who spend big money on art.

What is also factored in when discussing provenance are the stories that come along with it. If an interesting, and true story regarding the ownership of an artwork occurs then that adds to its allure and overall mystery. Maybe it was a painting that an artist did for a loved one, and they kept that work with them for the rest of their life. Or maybe another artwork was owned by a Jewish

1. Thornton, Sarah, "Rockefeller Rothko," line 1.

family during Nazi rule in Germany and they had to smuggle it out of the country. Historical stories like these are ones that help to prop up the artwork itself. Humans are a storytelling species, and what we hear matters to us. If there is a heart wrenching back-story to an artwork, then that piece typically gains a higher social importance, which equals a higher price tag. Much of Leonardo da Vinci's paintings have minimal backstory to them, and what we are left with are the notes that he was writing at the time he made it. And while we are able to gain a lot of knowledge regarding his thought process, we do not have specific, intimate moments of his life and how they directly relate to any particular painting of his.

If the *Salvator Mundi* had a decent provenance, then the controversy of who painted it would never have happened. In all fairness, many of the works by da Vinci do not have a strong provenance. He died with only three of his own paintings in his possession, and the rest of the works attributed to him go off of many other factors, provenance being only one of them. However, the chain of ownership for the *Salvator Mundi* is so weak that no reputable art scholar claims it is a driving factor in its attribution to da Vinci. We really only have a speculative understanding of the origins of the painting, with some people claiming that it was commissioned by Isabella d'Este, Duchess of Milan, for personal prayer. I have been unable to find concrete, or even wet concrete proof, that this commission actually occurred. There is speculation that Leonardo painted a version of a Salvator Mundi and that it was potentially destroyed or lost in 1603.[2] The question that remains is if this Salvator Mundi is the current one in question, or if da Vinci even painted a Salvator Mundi at all. It remains a mystery.

The painting may have been in the collection of James Hamilton, an English nobleman, from 1638–1641.[3] Hamilton was executed during the English Civil War in 1649, but that is a full 8 years after the possible date the painting would have left his collection. How the *Salvator Mundi* would have gotten into his possession remains unknown. In 1649, it entered Queen Henrietta Maria's

2. Marani, *Complete Paintings*, 340.

3. Cole, "Salvator Mundi," line 4.

collection, the same year her husband, King Charles I of England, Scotland, and Ireland was executed. The painting was then put up for sale by the English Commonwealth and it was bought by a creditor in 1651. It was then brought back to Charles II after the English Restoration in 1660. In 1666 it was included in Charles' inventory of possessions at the Palace of Whitehall. From there it would be inherited by James II, but after it enters his ownership the provenance once again gets murky. Some scholars believe that the *Salvator Mundi* stayed in his possession until he passed, but no one can be certain of this. And some think that the painting was given to his mistress, Catherine Sedley, however, this too is only speculation. The painting would then somehow be auctioned off by Sir Charles Herbert Sheffield, the illegitimate son of John Sheffield, 1st Duke of Buckingham and Normanby, in 1763.[4] We do not know who bought the painting during this sale. The work then eventually ended up in the ownership of Francis Cook, who was born in 1817, a full fifty-four years after the last known sale of the *Salvator Mundi*.

With this long list of supposed ownership of the *Salvator Mundi*, it must be pointed out that we are simply told to trust that the limited records we do have are talking about the painting in question. For all we know, Francis Cook could have purchased a different painting than what was listed in these old records. Francis Cook, 1st Viscount of Monserrate, was an English businessman and avid art collector. Born into wealth, he would go on to join his father's company, Cook, Son & Co., in which Francis Cook would eventually lead until his own passing in 1901. Cook, Son & Co. worked in the trade business that specialized in the wholesale of cloth, which made him to be one of Britain's richest men.[5] With his fortune, he bought hundreds of pieces of art, amassing quite a serious collection. And the *Salvator Mundi* was one of those artworks to have entered his collection. Cook purchased it one year before his death, in 1900.[6] Neither Francis Cook or any of

---

4. Daley, "Louvre Abu Dhabi," line 8.

5. Cumming, *My Dear BB*, 522.

6. Zöllner, *Leonardo*, 250.

his associates made the claim that the *Salvator Mundi* was done by Leonardo da Vinci.

Chapter 11: Other Suspects

The only way to truly become a better artist is to practice the craft. Reading vast materials, listening to lectures, and having conversations are great ways to understand art and how you wish to go about it. However, when push comes to shove, you must break out the paints and brushes and start giving it a go. Additionally, one of the best ways to improve skills as a painter is to copy from the masters. This practice has been going on for hundreds of years and has greatly improved work by artists. My own artistic practice involves copying other great artists to learn from them. It has been one of the best learning tools in my arsenal. With so many artists participating in copying as a main method to learn, we see similar styles of art and skill levels emerge from all of them. *Salvator Mundi* does not look to be that great or even that serious of a painting. I think that it is more likely a work by a student who is still practicing than it is of a legendary artist. There are other Salvator Mundis that were made around that time, and they are far superior in quality. In addition, there are several artists other than Leonardo da Vinci that could have been the hand behind this painting.

At the age of thirty-eight, in the year 1490, da Vinci was able to establish his workshop in Florence that would include his own assistant and students. Leonardeschi were the artists who worked in the studio of Leonardo da Vinci. Many talented artists perfected their craft and learned from the greatest in this workshop. Da Vinci's reach was so vast that the Leonardeschi identification extended beyond the Florentine border and spilled into other parts of Europe. The most prominent artists that took part in this workshop came from various regions, like Milan and Spain. And other Europeans, including the German artist, Albrecht Dürer, were inspired by not only what Leonardo was creating, but also by what was coming out of his workshop. This makes for a clear understanding that, like most other artists' workshops at the time, there was immense collaboration. It could be suggested then that many of the student's paintings very well could have a flick or two of paint on them that was done by Leonardo. Of course, we would not be able to tell which single paint stroke would have been done by him. It also certainly would not make the work attributable to da Vinci. Yet, it does insinuate the team effort that went into much of the paintings.

Scholars who attribute the *Salvator Mundi* to da Vinci lean heavily on the blessing right hand. This is a default example that they use whenever the issue of which paint strokes were done by him, and which were not. For the people who vote in the affirmative of its attribution to the polymath, they all find that the right hand was done in an extraordinary fashion. I tend to agree. The issue here still lies in that several students of his could have painted a hand like that. And quite frankly, other artists of the Renaissance could have painted hands that way too. But even if da Vinci were to have been the one to have painted the hand, it is such a small portion of the overall painting that it is simply not enough to attribute it to Leonardo. For people to confidently assert that this painting was completely done by Leonardo is not acceptable, especially when their only piece of strong evidence is that of a single hand. While I do not find the hand to be convincing evidence, attributing the painting to da Vinci's Workshop, with possible assistance from Leonardo, would be a much fairer title for the work.

Dr. Carmen Bambach, Head Curator at the Met Museum in New York City, is a talented art scholar and da Vinci expert. An immigrant who escaped the Chilean 1973 coup d'état as a girl, she would make her way to Yale University. While preparing for her senior thesis on the Sistine Chapel, Bambach came across a drawing by Michelangelo that he drew to prepare for the Chapel. Initially labeled as an armpit, Bambach turned the drawing upside-down and saw that it was actually a drawing of a part of the head of Haman, a biblical figure on the Sistine Chapel. Shortly after, she went to the Vatican and was brought up to the Chapel's ceiling where she would hold the drawing up to the face of Haman. It was a perfect match.[1] Bambach's extraordinary talent in her work with the Italian Renaissance is truly remarkable. In addition to this finding, and her curatorial position, she also published a four-volume set on Leonardo da Vinci titled, *Leonardo da Vinci Rediscovered*. Furthermore, she is publicly outspoken that the *Salvator Mundi* was not painted by da Vinci.

Considering the many talented students that da Vinci had in his workshop, the *Salvator Mundi* could seamlessly be attributed to one of them instead. Dr. Carmen Bambach attributes the painting to Giovanni Boltraffio, a student of Leonardo's.[2] Examining the works of Boltraffio, you can see that he utilizes the *Chiaroscuro* technique. This is a method that shows the heavy use of light and shadow, usually as a black background, as seen with the *Salvator Mundi*. His *Portrait of a Young Man, possibly Girolamo Casio*, in the year 1500, shows a great comparison between itself and the *Salvator Mundi*. The locks of hair are much more in sync with one another. You can also find other striking resemblances, like the crooked nose and the ends of the figure's lips that slightly droop. Giovanni Boltraffio is a prime example of the crossover between students and teachers regarding their stylistic pursuits. Boltraffio's painting, *Madonna Litta*, was attributed for many years to having been done by da Vinci's hand. Conclusive evidence exists now that this painting is that of Giovanni's. Questions of attribution, and Boltraffio's overall style resembling the *Salvator Mundi*, make for a strong case by Carmen Bambach.

Not much is known about Giovanni Boltraffio; however, we know he was a faithful student of da Vinci who incorporated many of the same techniques. This is a primary reason why many people think of him as the one who painted the *Salvator Mundi*. Giorgio

1. Vilcek, "Renaissance Woman," lines 5–7.
2. Brown, "Leonardo Expert," line 2.

Vasari famously wrote that Boltraffio came from a wealthy, aristo-cratic family. Without diving too deeply into speculation, a person from an aristocratic family who became an artist in those times usually meant that they exhibited a deep, unavoidable skill at their craft. This is certainly evident in the paintings that he created. Bol-traffio consistently utilized techniques like *chiaroscuro* with a solid black background in many of his paintings. This echoes the *Salva-dor Mundi* and further strengthens the case that he is a more likely candidate as the artist of the work. *Portrait of a Young Woman with a Scorpion Chain,* a painting attributed to Giovanni Boltraffio, uses not only a black background, but has similarly styled designs on the woman's clothing. It also has similar shading techniques to that of the *Salvator Mundi.*

Dr. Matthew Landrus, University of Oxford, ascribes the *Salvator Mundi* to another one of da Vinci's students, Bernardino Luini.[3] When reviewing the paintings made by Luini, it is easy to tell that he worked directly with Leonardo. There is a bright, hon-est light that radiates from the faces of the people in his paintings, much like that of da Vinci's. The creamy, almost three-dimensional shape of the bodies comes out from the canvas and subtlety tricks the eye into believing for a time that you are looking at a real hu-man. The similar style that the two artists share can be seen in examples of collating Luini's *Saint Catherine* and da Vinci's *La Belle Ferronnière.* Furthermore, Bernardino Luini's Jesus in the painting, *Christ Among the Doctors,* looks nearly identical to the *Salvator Mundi.* This painting was started around the year 1515 and completed around 1530. This suggests that Luini could have painted the *Salvator Mundi* and then created the painting *Christ Among the Doctors* using a similar looking Jesus. It has always been common for artists to work with a running theme of familiar figures. It is plausible that the Jesus between these two paintings is part of a theme for him.

Little is known about Luini's life. But a concrete fact about him that we do know is that he was a student in several differ-ent artist workshops. He also painted a few frescos. An essential

3. Neuendorf, "Leonardo's Assistant," line 2.

aspect to understanding Luini is that his artistic methods shifted over time. We can tell from looking at his artworks chronologically that his skills also progressed over his lifetime. Later on in his life he became fascinated by the style of Raphael, and this is evident in his later fresco, *Jesus Among the Doctors*. He had such an uncanny ability to shift his own artistic focus to then blend in like a chameleon with the popular techniques at the time. This makes for yet another strong argument that he also could have been the man who painted the *Salvator Mundi*. The paintings Luini was making show that he mastered not only the style of the period, but that he could morph an image into whatever he wished it to be.

Whoever makes the claim is then responsible for providing the evidence for their assertion. The evidence that Leonardo da Vinci painted the *Salvator Mundi* is minimal on an unconvincing level. Just because some parts of the painting look like it was made by someone with talent does not mean that the talent was from da Vinci. His students, and other artists of the time, carried the capability to paint something like the *Salvator Mundi*. Artists like Boltraffio and Luini are much more reasonable options as the author behind the work. The painting was not only created at a time when Leonardo was at the height of his artistic abilities, but it was also at a time when the competition was high due to the rise of Michelangelo and Raphael. Examining paintings done by Boltraffio and Luini shows a particular style that much better matches the painting than da Vinci's style does. And it must keep on being said that top da Vinci scholars do not attribute this painting to him; only a relatively small number of da Vinci experts make the claim that they think he is the one who painted it. Nonetheless, there are many moving parts to the *Salvator Mundi*, and those moving parts involve dangerous, powerful people.

Chapter 12: Copy Cats

The best way for an artist to learn is by attempting to copy great works of art. Spending time with a painting allows the student to learn how it was made, such as which colors were blended for each part. A student can pick up the particular rhythm of the artist and the types of brushes they used all by the flow of the painting itself. Roy Lichtenstein, for example, preferred to use thick black lines and colorful dot patterns to make up his comic-style paintings. People who are studying art focus on things like this in his works, such as the width of blank spaces between the dots, as well as the dot size itself. Painting is always in the details. Even total abstract artists like Jackson Pollock utilized a very sophisticated flow with the work that he made. Art students copying older paintings is a very old and proven practice because it is a surefire way for them to improve their own skills. Another important aspect of copying a painting is that you can learn new techniques that you may not have known before. Great artists tend to have methods that can be valuable to someone who is learning.

Many believe the Louvre to have been the first museum to have an official Copyist program, first allowing these artists to create work in 1793. Back in this time, and through the 1800s, there was no limit to the number of people, regardless of skill level, that could paint inside the museum. The Louvre would even provide everyone with their own easel to borrow while they were there.[1] This, however, would go away as the program became

---

1. Wright, "Copyists," 116.

more popular. The Louvre is secretive about how exactly they run their Copyist department, but it is thought that they only allow 150–250 artists a year into their official program. With thousands of requests each year, the Louvre selects this limited number of artists based on their skill level and the proposal of the work they wish to copy. Once selected, the artist must provide several forms of identity verification, and then they receive the coveted permit allowing them to paint in the museum. Most of these permits are written for three months, and the artist can request extra time if it does not interfere with the functioning of the museum. The application for myself to be a Copyist was not necessarily grueling, but there were many detailed parts that were needed.

Over the years, other high-profile museums have adopted their own Copyist programs that are also limited and based on merit. A couple museums with these programs are the MET in Manhattan, as well as the Prado Museum in Madrid. The Prado Museum made news headlines in November 2021 when they made the public declaration that they did not think that Leonardo da Vinci painted the *Salvator Mundi*. The museum reached this conclusion when preparing for a da Vinci exhibition titled *Leonardo and the copy of the Mona Lisa. New approaches to the artist's studio practices*, in which they had collaborated with other notable institutions such as the Louvre, National Gallery in London, as well as the Molecular Archaeology Laboratory at the Sorbonne. In this exhibition, the museum labeled the *Salvator Mundi* as being by his workshop, not by the artist himself. The Prado Museum has since maintained that while they do not attribute this painting to da Vinci, they think he painted another Salvator Mundi.[2] However, if da Vinci painted another version of a Salvator Mundi, then it would look very different than the one in question.

The question of forgeries can come up when describing a Copyist program. *What if they swap it out for the original? What if they try to sell it off as the real thing?* These are valid questions, but what needs to be remembered is that these museums have entire departments devoted to their Copyist programs. When I was

---

2. Bailey, "Prado," line 1.

granted the permit from the Louvre, they obtained copies of my passport and driver's license. So, they not only had all my contact information, email, and image, but also my official US citizen papers. If I were to have done something wrong in there, I would have immediately been apprehended. Another way that they prevent forgeries is that the artist must use a smaller size canvas than the original painting, and the Copyist is not allowed to sign the painting with the original artist's name. Instead, the artist must sign their own name on the work they created. For larger paintings, the work needs to be inspected by someone in the Copyist department, and then the back of the painting is stamped three times with the Louvre's official seal. The Copyist is then escorted out of the museum by an employee with their painting to ensure that no guards attempt to stop them from leaving.

Henri Matisse, Pablo Picasso, and Paul Cézanne are just a few of the historical artists who were Copyists at the Louvre. A famous quote from Cézanne is when he described the Louvre as a book that artists learn how to read. In addition to being difficult to have the Louvre see an artist as being worthy enough for one of their Copyist permits, it is also a challenge to settle on which artwork to choose if selected. The Louvre owns hundreds of thousands of works of art and objects. This makes for an overwhelming decision of what to copy and provides artists with a sea of knowledge they need to obtain. Pablo Picasso led an extraordinary artistic life in his own right. From being a Copyist at the Louvre to then being the richest living artist at the time, he proved his tenacity and commitment to the arts. Picasso passed away at the age of ninety-one in 1973. It was in 1971, that the Louvre displayed his artwork inside their museum, alongside paintings by the Old Masters. In addition, the Louvre collected several works of art by Picasso for its permanent collection. He was an artist that came a long way from being a Copyist at the Louvre to having his own exhibition and artwork collected by the same museum.

With the Louvre's Copyist program being so wildly popular, the selected artists generally must be put on a waitlist that can range anywhere from one to two years. Between the length of the waitlist and then the typical time commitment of 3 months to copy a work of art, many of the people are local Parisians. However, it is a dream for many artists to be accepted into the program, and it is common to see people take a sabbatical from their jobs and temporarily move to Paris to pursue this. My trip to Paris with my wife, Erin, was already booked when I decided to apply for the program. So, spending three months creating a rendition of an artwork was not an option. I explained this to the Louvre's Copyist Department when applying. They were kind enough to not only make an exception for the length of copying, but they also moved me up the waitlist so that I would be able to do my work in time. Although I never officially found out their generous reasoning behind this, I am only to assume that it is because of my professional background as an artist.

There is so much rejection in the art world that it is easy to become discouraged. That is why when artists build up enough vision and talent, they come to a crossroads of either maintaining art as a personal hobby or getting their work out there into the world. If they end up choosing to put their work out there for galleries and collectors to see, then they usually come up against almost immediate rejection. Even the biggest names in art today still get rejected. What matters is if the artist has thick enough skin to keep pushing forward and improving their skills. Often these rejections come in the form of never giving a response to the artist. That is why it can be a good sign to receive a written rejection from a gallery or institution because it means they at least respect the artist's work enough to write back. The Copyist Department at the Louvre is an example of an institution that typically does not send rejection letters. In a way, most of my worth as an artist came to me after I received the acceptance letter from the Louvre in June 2022 because it acknowledged that I had what it takes. Being an official Copyist at the Louvre is an honor and comes with a high level of responsibility.

Chapter 13: Up for the Task

It is hard to go to Paris and not feel inspired. The architecture, the smell of bread from the bakeries, and the endless amount of beautiful art are just some things that make up this great city. If in New York anything is possible, then Paris makes it known that *you* are possible. The City of Lights is one of the only places away from my actual home where I truly also feel at home. I have been fortunate enough to have been to many places around the world. From Mexico and Colombia, down to Argentina, and across the Pacific Ocean to the jungles of northern Vietnam and the crowded provinces of China. But my heart and mind always return to Paris. I improve my creative vision while there, and I am sure that drinking espressos in the cafés and overindulging in Champagne helps to play a role. It makes my Copyist endeavor in the Louvre all the more worthwhile. I was finally back in the European city that I love. Erin and I even got to spend a couple of days there with our good friends, who happened to be vacationing in Paris as well.

The Louvre was even busier since the last time I was there, which was about eight years prior. Tickets were booked a couple of months in advance, and I was able to secure a Monday with their second earliest time available at 9:30 am. My advice for anyone wanting to visit the Louvre is to go on a weekday, preferably not in high season, and reserve the earliest time slot that you can. Once inside the museum, go straight for the *Mona Lisa*, and ignore everything else until you have seen her. It does not take long at all for the line to see her grow to great lengths. Once you have witnessed the painting, go and see the rest of the museum. You will thank me later if you follow those easy instructions. The Louvre is filled daily with tens of thousands of visitors, so the more time you can spend inside this museum with fewer crowds of people, the better. Earlier time entries make for a more pleasant experience. Going to the most popular museum in the world in the summertime, on a weekend, in the middle of the day, will make for a more stressful outing.

Anyone who visits the Louvre is allowed to bring a small sketchbook with a graphite pencil so that they can practice their drawings. Since its inception, the Louvre has always been a place for artists to not only admire the work inside, but to also practice their own skills. It is the Copyist permit that artists envy as this not only allows them to bring paints and brushes inside, but it also allows them to bring in larger canvases. The permit is also the official nod of approval from the Louvre itself that essentially says that they see you as a worthwhile artist. It is vindication at its finest. I could have brought in dozens of paints and a full set of brushes, but I wanted to move about the museum freely. So, bringing in less materials would work better for myself. More importantly, capturing the essence of Leonardo da Vinci was much more of an interest to me than seeing if using Cadmium Red or Cobalt Blue could be uniquely incorporated into the painting. I wanted to do the painting justice, not satisfy my own ego by using flamboyant colors.

Opting to use minimal materials to create my rendition of *Saint John the Baptist* had me feeling pensive and adaptable. Looking back, I can tell that if I chose to use more colors and various materials, it would seem more like a chore. And honestly, I do not think that my painting would have turned out the way I needed it to. My multiple paper canvases (always come prepared with backups), three paintbrushes, and charcoal paint were the only needed items. This was the material that I had practiced with countless times. These items were ones that I grew accustomed to using and was the material that I felt could best speak to the work of Leonardo da Vinci in a contemporary manner in the year 2022. I kept Erin's voice in my head. Her reassurance of my skills as an artist and her insight that the Louvre selected me because they believe in me, helped a great deal. They did not want me to pretend to be da Vinci; they wanted my own voice as the interpretation of da Vinci, as she said to me. All of the work I had poured in as an artist over the years had brought me to that present moment. This was the time for me to paint in front of legends.

Priority was to first see the *Mona Lisa*. If we had delayed seeing her, the line to get up close to the painting for viewing would have been frustratingly long. I am not a patient person. With our early reservation time at the Louvre, the line to view the painting was less than 5 minutes; no patience required. This is another benefit to using minimal materials there because I was able to keep the paint brushes in my pockets and then easily carry the thin canvases. We were both teary-eyed once we got up close to the *Mona Lisa* because of her ultimate magnificence. She has such a radiant brilliance that we were overcome with emotion. The power of this image speaks for not only art, but also human existence. She pulls you in with confident strength. This painting is truly the apex of human creativity. A masterpiece. A revelation. Leonardo da Vinci created the ultimate image, which is truly perfect in every way.

The Director who wrote my permit instructed me to show it to one of the guards before beginning my work. But there was something about the permit that looked like there may have been more to it than just being able to copy *Saint John the Baptist*. So, after viewing the *Mona Lisa*, I wondered to myself if maybe this permit would also work on that painting. The worst they could tell me was *no*. So, after viewing the *Mona Lisa*, I showed the guard next to the painting my Copyist permit. Upon inspection, his eyes became very big, and in English, he looked at me and said, "Right this way." The kind guard then allowed me to remain inside the famed room, the Salle des États, where the *Mona Lisa* resides, and brought me up close to her. It had then become apparent to me that the Director of the Louvre wrote my permit in a way that allowed me to also create my own rendition of Leonardo da Vinci's *Mona Lisa*. I had no time to think. Just time to act. With this rush of emotions, I began to paint my copy of her.

With the room full of visitors waiting in line to get up close to the *Mona Lisa*, there I was, with a guard by my side, painting my own version. I blocked out the excited noise from the crowd and remained focused on the *Mona Lisa* and how I was to go about the painting. I focused on the rivers and roads behind Lisa Gherardini, who is thought to be the woman in the painting. I kept in mind that the landscape alludes to the female body, and she is just as much a part of the environment as the environment is a part of her. And I went about my depiction by incorporating exaggerated shades to pay homage to the sfumato technique. The famous smile on her is something that I knew I had to get right, but within a more abstract and contemporary context. With a pencil, I lightly made the smile, and then, with the charcoal paint and brush, I calmly smoothed it out. This was to magnify da Vinci's brilliant use of shading and blending of tones that illuminates his skill. While painting, it felt like I was the only person in the room with her.

The canvas I had selected for the paintings was smooth but left enough grab to it so the charcoal paint could have a more raw appearance rather than a flushed out, flat look. The harder I pressed down on my paintbrush, the denser the charcoal appeared. Easing up on the brush left a grayish hue, while being even lighter with the brush created an almost silver-like look. This was expected after months of preparation, but I had not prepared to use these techniques in recreating the *Mona Lisa*. What became immediately apparent to me was that I had to be intentional with the landscape behind her. The rivers and roads, and mountains and valleys, all allude to the natural beauty of the figure. And, of course, I could not ignore the most famous smile in the world. I lightly flicked the charcoal paint in such a way as to make a lighthearted image of the smile, and just like da Vinci, I added layer upon layer to the lips. Without worrying about trying to make an exact copy of her, I made a contemporary version of her. Whimsical swifts of charcoal paint and respectful maneuvering of the brush led me to my own rendition. The shock of the Louvre authorizing me to paint the *Mona Lisa* did not really hit me until later that night.

When I completed that painting, I thanked the guard and walked over to Erin, whose face and eyes showed both shock and excitement about what I was allowed to do. But there was still one more painting that I needed to take on, *Saint John the Baptist*. For this rendition, I opted to do a triptych, which is when three separate paintings are created and meant to all be displayed together. The first painting would have a more realistic look, like da Vinci's painting. The second one would still incorporate realistic elements, but have my own abstractions added. And the third would be an almost total abstract presentation, with elements of familiarity to the original. As with the *Mona Lisa*, the room became incredibly crowded. There was no choice but to stay focused on my task at hand, block out distractions, and do what I came there to do. The charcoal paint glided across the canvas. The silver hues would shade over into gray and then to black. And in what seemed like the blink of an eye, the three paintings of *Saint John the Baptist* were completed. The metaphorical weight I felt on my shoulders and mind had been lifted. My work was finished. Despite minor areas that I would need to touch up when I returned to the US, there was no more work that I needed to do in the Louvre Museum. The rest of my time inside was spent admiring the works of art on display.

Right after I completed the last brush stroke in the museum, the noise that I had been able to block out had suddenly returned. The whirlwind of the experience of being allowed to paint there had now settled me back to reality. It was still early in the day, and there was still so much more to see. We made our way through the many halls, admiring the masterpieces surrounding us. The Louvre felt like home. You could be looking at a remarkable painting and then look up at the ceiling to discover that, it too, was painted by another great artist. No one needs to be a connoisseur of the arts to understand that they are surrounded by true greatness. The magnificence of the palace and the art itself makes me tremble and feel glad to be alive. The Louvre brings out the motivations for living a good life and having a life worth living. I feel nothing but gratefulness that the Louvre deemed me worthy enough to bring in brushes to create my own paintings. I was walking with giants and painting with gods.

After spending hours in the Louvre, we returned to the flat we were staying in to drop off my paintings. Having built up an appetite, we went out for a meal, and both got Croque-Madames at a nearby café. There was an adorable French bulldog who was there with its owner, so we spent much of our time there giving the dog head scratches and belly rubs. While eating, it started to downpour, but Paris is always beautiful in the rain. Once the showers stopped, we spent the rest of the day wandering the streets of Paris. Stopping by cafés for an espresso or two, and then ending up at another spot for an Aperol Spritz. We admired the cobblestone streets we walked on and were infatuated with the designs carved into many of the old buildings. In fact, much of our time in Paris was spent walking. Late into the night we returned to our flat, and it was at that moment when the shock of painting in the Louvre wore off. I realized, in a full state of mind, that *I had painted in the Louvre*. I immediately embraced my wife and told her, "Thank you for always believing in me."

Chapter 14: A Lovely Smile

On May 29, 2022, a man disguised as an older woman in a wheelchair got up close to the *Mona Lisa* and threw a mushy handful of cake at her. He was swiftly manhandled away by security while shouting about changes to the earth's climate. The climate activist was escorted out of the Louvre and sent to a psychiatric unit for a mental health evaluation.[1] Fortunately, the *Mona Lisa* is behind bullet-proof glass, so the only thing that needed to happen was to use window cleaner on the protective barrier to wipe it off. This incident was not an isolated one, as other climate activists have targeted other great works of art to help promote their agenda. Two girls threw cold tomato soup at one of Vincent van Gogh's *Sunflower* paintings, then proceeded to glue themselves to the wall in which the work hung. Another group even threw mashed potatoes at a landscape painting by Claude Monet, and of course, they too glued themselves to the wall. Those are unfortunately not the only incidents of climate activists attacking important works of art; however, the good news is that these paintings were not damaged due to the shielding glass.

This is also not the first time, and probably not the last time, that the *Mona Lisa* has been attacked. In 1956, a man threw rocks at her, and in 2009 a woman launched a teacup at the painting. These are just a few examples of violent attacks on this work of art over the years. The painting was also stolen. Back on August 22, 1911, a Louvre Copyist named Louis Béroud went to the museum

1. Torchinsky, "Piece of Cake," lines 1–5.

to create his own rendition of the *Mona Lisa*. The only problem was that when he went to the room to paint her, he noticed it was not there. Béroud notified the guards, who initially believed it to be with the museum's photography department. Eventually they realized that the painting had been stolen. The Louvre closed down for an entire week while a formal investigation took place. This investigation would even lead to Pablo Picasso as a suspect. Picasso did not steal the Mona Lisa, and he was not involved in any way with its theft. However, he was not necessarily completely innocent in matters related to stolen art. Picasso stole two Iberian statues from the Louvre around the same time the *Mona Lisa* taken. Pablo Picasso was arrested and charged with stealing the statues, but ultimately the case was dismissed. He walked away a free man, and all charges were dropped.[2]

It turns out that the theft of the painting was an inside job, stolen by an employee at the Louvre. Twenty-nine-year-old, Vincenzo Peruggia, stole the painting and brought it back to Italy, where he believed it belonged. This Italian nationalist was able to successfully get the artwork out of the museum and into his Parisian apartment, where it would stay hidden away for two years. After this time, Peruggia transported the work to Italy, where he contacted an art expert, Mario Fratelli, in Florence. Fratelli authenticated the artwork alongside art expert, Giovanni Poggi, and both men then contacted local authorities who arrested Peruggia. When on trial, the court agreed that Peruggia committed the theft out of his own perceived patriotic duty and sentenced him to jail for one year and fifteen days. He only ended up serving about seven months of his sentence before being released.[3] Some people claim that it is events such as this that led to the popularity of the *Mona Lisa*. But what they do not realize is that events such as this theft, and later attacks on it, occurred because the painting is itself a true masterpiece. And in my opinion, the greatest work of art to ever exist.

2. Chua-Eoan, "Top 25 Crimes," line 1.
3. Charney, "History and Thefts," line 3.

A common thing that I hear people say after viewing the *Mona Lisa* is that they couldn't believe how small it actually is. While this misconception runs rampant through social media and dinner parties, the painting is fairly large when compared to other half-length portraits of the Renaissance.[4] Coming in at thirty inches × twenty-one inches, it may be smaller than some contemporary art we see, but all in all, it is of a larger scale when considering the time in which it was painted. It is now widely accepted that the *Mona Lisa,* also referred to as *La Joconde* by the French, was a commissioned portrait of a woman named Lisa del Giocondo. She was a member of the Gherardini family and an Italian noblewoman. Her husband, Francesco di Bartolomeo di Zanobi del Giocondo, was a successful merchant who dabbled in various types of trade that were quite profitable. While he was not on the same level as other powerful families, such as the Medici family, he made enough to own a large villa with multiple farms located on expensive land just outside of Florence. He was also a patron of the arts, and one of his requested commissions was to build a chapel with Christian iconography. Francesco Giocondo would also be the one to commission Leonardo da Vinci to do the portrait of his wife.[5]

Despite this painting originally being a commission, Leonardo ends up holding onto it and continuously works on it for the rest of his life. Over these years he made small, delicate changes that would ultimately create a masterpiece. He ends up putting all his talents into this one image, perfecting every aspect of the painting. It looks like it was almost as if da Vinci was testing himself and pushing his own limits on the artwork. Leonardo da Vinci viewed art as the same thing as science and engineering, they were all one and the same to him. His extensive notes on the physical nature of light and shading come through in the portrait that helps to further prove this point. The angular structures throughout the *Mona Lisa* are all scientifically correct according to the positioning of the forms in the painting. Da Vinci did not simply look to show lightness and darkness in the work, but to focus in on how

4. Kemp, *Living with Leonardo*, 72.
5. Aspen Institute, "Martin Kemp," 11:36.

shade tends to have a bleeding effect as it forms off the curvatures of structures. A strong example of this is the veil that she wears. You see the border of it, but you can still also see her forehead through the veil. The veil then becomes more of a gray tone as it goes over her hair. This is an exact depiction of what wearing a thin veil would look like on an actual person. The *Salvator Mundi* painting does not show this level of understanding of light, darkness, and shade at all.

Part of Leonardo da Vinci's studies is his work on optics. He understood that the eye is a profound instrument that carries a great deal of complexity. Through his sketches and notes, we see that he discovered that the eye does not see the edges of any structure. Instead, the focus from the eyes adjusts to the distance of what it is looking at while it moves around through its peripherals instead. There are no hard lines with the vision of the eye, and that is why da Vinci painted this way in his artistic career. There are no lines anywhere to be found on the *Mona Lisa*; instead, he paints each figure in the same way as the human eye would see it. His studies of water and how it swirled around were another influence in his paintings. As with the *Mona Lisa*, her hair has a natural balance and movement to it, like how swirls of water naturally pass by. The hair falls in a way that is appropriate with the pull of gravity to the mass of her hair. Details mattered very much to Leonardo da Vinci.

In one of his scientific notebooks, Leonardo writes about the earth as being connected to humans. He writes that soil is like flesh, rivers are of blood, our cartilage is the rocks, so on and so forth. Da Vinci sees the earth as another living form with many semblances to that of our own human bodies. He also does complex drawings of the insides of humans, including one of a woman. This shows the veins and valves, and how they function. These drawings go hand in hand with how he views the natural world around him. Everything has a purpose, everything is connected. For a mind like Leonardo, he needed to understand the interior and how it relates to what we see on the exterior. Whether it is the inner workings of our bodies and how it forms what we see, or how a woman's hair rests under a veil. He paints Lisa del Giocondo not as being in a landscape but rather as being the landscape itself.[6]

Today the *Mona Lisa* remains housed in the Salle des États room in the Louvre. In the past, she has been brought out on tour, like in 1963 when it was presented in Washington D.C. And also to New York, and then Japan and Russia in 1974. With the age of this work, it is unlikely that it will ever leave the walls of the Louvre again; however, anything is possible. But, as of this moment, it rests behind a thick protective glass, with guards by its side, and is illuminated by a unique LED lighting that was made specifically for the artwork.[7] It is rarely taken out of its frame, and only done so for inspections and to assess its physical state.[8] So far, there have not been too many concerning issues with the delicate artwork. To put a price point on such an object would be an incredibly difficult task to take on. However, if someone was willing to pay $450.3 million for a subpar painting that was irresponsibly attributed to da Vinci, you can then only imagine the monetary value of the *Mona Lisa*. What we do know is that millions of people have visited this extraordinary masterpiece, and she is always there, smiling back at us.

---

6. Kemp, *Living with Leonardo*, 76–7.
7. Fontoynont, "Lighting Mona Lisa," line 1.
8. Kemp, *Living with Leonardo*, 70.

Chapter 15: How Much?

Despite years of restorative work by Dianne Modestini, a few more steps needed to be taken before a sale could take place. Even when considering her impressive credentials, she alone could not have the sole authority to attribute the artwork to a specific creator. And with a lack of provenance, there needed to be a consensus of Leonardo da Vinci scholars making congruent assertions that he painted the *Salvator Mundi*. I believe it to be the case that Alexander Parish and Robert Simon, owners of the painting, thought early on that the painting was done by a great artist. The two of them eagerly agreed with Modestini's assessment that it was painted by da Vinci. It would be hard to have a different reaction if a well-respected art restorer makes a claim such as this one. However, there was a clear bias from the people selling the work because of their financial interests. Having Modestini in their corner was a great start for them, but they would need more.

Over the years, there have been many people that have made outlandish claims involving artworks by Leonardo da Vinci. Martin Kemp, one of the foremost da Vinci scholars, has stated in interviews that he has come across people asking him to verify ungrounded theories they have about the artist.[1] Many of these peculiar theories involve elements that would not make sense for an artist of the Renaissance to do. An example being that the artist left coded messages underneath a painted picture. The clear issue with this is why would an artist from more than five hundred

1. Auction Podcast, "Martin Kemp," 35:09.

82

years ago leave a code that could only be detected with the modern technology of today? With all this being said, who wouldn't want to make a discovery involving Leonardo da Vinci? It is an alluring thought. So being presented with a painting that, on the surface, appears to have similar markings of a Leonardo, and most likely came right out of his workshop, is a surefire way to have your name be added in the art history books. The desire to make a forever-changing discovery can creep into our own subconscious. That is why it is important to continue to note that I do not think everyone involved in attributing the *Salvator Mundi* to da Vinci did so with malicious intentions. Some certainly did. But maybe the others were just looking for their own treasure hunt, and the historical awards that would be granted to them.

Parish and Simon could not simply put the *Salvator Mundi* up for sale or auction with only Modestini's assessment of it. There are rules that need to be followed. A lack of provenance and a positive view from one art specialist is not enough to set out for a buyer. They would need a small army of scholars backing them. That way, if any doubts are raised after the painting is sold, they could simply point to the list of important people who made their professional opinion known. Without that support, you could be looking at a string of life-ruining lawsuits. But what you can do is use the backing of several scholars to your advantage. You get enough of the right people in your corner, then suddenly it doesn't matter that other scholars of equal footing on the other side of the issue exist. Naysayers can be written off once an official standard has been set. And credit needs to be given to Parish and Simon because not only did they follow the needed formula for this painting's attribution, but moved quickly enough to not give other scholars a chance to dispute its authenticity.

After Dianne Modestini's restoration and attributing it to da Vinci, Parish and Simon then paraded it around. It would be sent off for private tours to the Metropolitan Museum of Art, as well as the Museum of Fine Arts in Boston, so curators could preview the work in person. The most contentious moment of this secretive tour was when they brought it to the National Gallery in London, inviting five well-respected Leonardo da Vinci scholars to view it. Upon examination by these academics, the owners of the *Salvator Mundi* suggested that all of them agreed that the *Salvator Mundi* was, in fact, done by the polymath.[2] With Dianne Modestini stating her belief that it is an authentic Leonardo, and now these other scholars saying it was also painted by him, then this makes for a strong case regarding its authenticity. The problem that arises here is that not all five of the scholars actually agreed to its authenticity, and a vote never took place about it either.

The five da Vinci scholars who viewed the *Salvator Mundi* in London at the National Gallery were Maria Teresa Fiorio, who has written several books on the Renaissance. Pietro Marani, who oversaw the restoration of Leonardo da Vinci's mural, *The Last Supper*. Carmen C. Bambach, the Curator of Drawings and Paintings at the Metropolitan Museum of Art (The MET). Martin Kemp, a da Vinci scholar at Oxford University. And David Alan Brown, Curator of Italian Paintings, National Gallery of Art, Washington, D.C. They each viewed the *Salvator Mundi* up close and walked away without agreeing on who could have painted this picture.[3] A far cry from the unanimous decision that was suggested to have taken place. Only two of these people would claim that Leonardo was the hand behind this painting, while the other three scholars did not attribute the painting to him. While two affirmatives make for a more stable case, it does not address the other three who disagree with that assessment.

These scholars would have their own mixed reactions after they viewed the *Salvator Mundi* in the flesh. Regarding their specific opinions on attribution, David Alan Brown and Martin Kemp said they believed it to have been painted by Leonardo. Maria Teresa Fiorio and Pietro Marani would not comment either way. And Carmen Bambach said that it was not painted by da Vinci.[4] The two no comments show that its authenticity can be interpreted in many ways, but at the end of the day, they would refuse to make

2. Vitkine, *Savior for Sale*, 16:25.
3. Koefoed, *The Lost Leonardo*, 22:50.
4. Vitkine, *Savior for Sale*, 1:21:35.

the claim that it was done by Leonardo. I read the no comments as flat-out disagreeing with it being done by da Vinci. Staying neutral on the matter shows that Fiorio and Marani did not want to make the leap of going on the record to say it was done by Leonardo. Bambach would be bold in her assertion by giving a direct and unfavorable view of what Kemp and Brown believe the painting to be. All five of them seemed to be impressed with the blessing right hand, but they needed to be more impressed for a full consensus of attribution to the polymath. Nevertheless, Parish and Simon carried on with their march towards the auction house and play down the mixed reviews from London. It must be noted that as time has passed, Pietro Marani has since stated his own reservations about the *Salvator Mundi* being attributed to Leonardo da Vinci, according to Dianne Modestini.[5] Fiorio later went on to publicly reaffirm that she never attributed the painting to Leonardo.[6]

To further help Parish and Simon's case for the *Salvator Mundi*, they were able to convince Luke Syson, curator at the National Gallery, to include the painting in an upcoming da Vinci show, *Leonardo Da Vinci: Painter at the Court of Milan*. This exhibition lasted from November 2011 to February 2012. The scandal here is that museums are not supposed to display artworks that are about to go on the market for sale. There are major ethical breaches by doing so because any work that displays at a museum, especially one on the level of the National Gallery, will increase its value and erase any doubts about its authenticity. Nevertheless, the painting was included in the exhibition. It was one of the biggest, most visited Leonardo da Vinci shows ever put on. Crowds of people swarmed outside as they eagerly awaited entry to see the many works. It was a major success for the National Gallery and surely brought in a ton of revenue for the museum. When the *Salvator Mundi* was on display there, they listed the painting as having been done solely by Leonardo da Vinci, with no studio participation.[7] A painting

---

5. Modestini, "History of the Salvator Mundi," line 13.

6. Cascone, "Contentious Takeaways," line 23.

7. Vitkine, *Savior for Sale*, 20:08.

based on only half-truths and unethical business practices meant that it was time to officially put the *Salvator Mundi* up for sale.

At first, Parish and Simon looked to sell the painting to a museum. None would bite, even with the assistance of art dealer Warren Adelson, whom they brought in for assistance with the sale.[8] Museums, even the well-funded ones with big-time donors, usually don't have the kind of cash available to purchase works of this magnitude. Maybe they can purchase artwork at a discount, but usually, they rely on donations. If you look through most art museums' lists of works in their collection, they have a brief blurb about the person or family that donated the work to them. Yes, the person donating gets a substantial tax write-off, but the museum also gets to now own a work that they otherwise would not have been able to afford. So, with the *Salvator Mundi*, it is not necessarily the case that they did not want it in their collections, but more so the case that they do not have deep enough pockets. Remember, this painting was also just coming off a hot streak with it being suggested that five da Vinci scholars believed in its authenticity. It also had its grand public showing at the National Gallery. But with no museums able to buy the work directly from them, they now needed to make this a public sale to whoever was willing to pay up.

In 2013, Sotheby's Auction House would approach Parish and Simon, saying that they had a buyer for the *Salvator Mundi*. This potential buyer was the Swiss art dealer and businessman Yves Bouvier. He was someone who inherited his father's storage company and later expanded them into what is known as freeports.[9] These high-tech facilities are essentially well-protected, climate-controlled safes that are used to store valuable goods. They are usually located in countries that allow the owners of the product to keep, buy, and sell their items without having to pay taxes. Much of the art that is sold at big-time auction houses go immediately into storage at one of these freeports. The owner is then able to do future sales of the art without needing to pay any taxes to the government. Millionaires and billionaires utilize these

8. Vitkine, *Savior for Sale*, 30:32.

9. Vitkine, *Savior for Sale*, 35:17.

freeports to help maximize various existing tax loopholes.[10] This is also a primary reason why art sells for such exorbitant prices.

In addition to his business ventures with freeports, Yves Bouvier also began acting as an art dealer of sorts to the Russian oligarch, Dmitry Rybolovlev. There was supposed to be an agreed-upon understanding between the two that Bouvier would locate and buy works of art for Rybolovlev. Bouvier would then sell the art to Rybolovlev for a 2% commission fee. The problem that arises here is that it appears Bouvier was lying about the cost of most of these artworks and was getting a much larger commission payment from the oligarch. Sotheby's was involved in brokering several of these deals that Bouvier spearheaded. The most famous artwork in question was the *Salvator Mundi*, which Bouvier bought for eighty million dollars, then immediately sold it to Rybolovlev for $127.5 million. Much higher than the 2% commission fee that Yves Bouvier was supposed to charge. It later became public knowledge that the oligarch was the owner of the painting, and it wasn't much longer after that when he found out about the markup from his art dealer. This has led to a series of lawsuits known collectively as the *Bouvier Affair*, which is still ongoing. It is also important to note that after Parish and Simon sold the painting to Bouvier, they gave Dianne Modestini a large, undisclosed sum of money.[11]

Dmitry Rybolovlev was beyond angry at the fraud that had taken place, so in addition to the various lawsuits he has put forward, he also put much of his art collection up for sale.[12] Staring at the artwork that you severely overpaid for would not sit well with anyone, including a billionaire. However, it was the *Salvator Mundi* painting that would most likely have the biggest potential for a substantial monetary gain. After all, this was thought to be an authentic painting by Leonardo da Vinci, and the only one in private hands. But if Rybolovlev purchased it from Bouvier for $127.5 million, he would need to find someone innovative, and with strong ties to the art market, to make him a profit. With the assistance

10. Vitkine, *Savior for Sale*, 35:38.
11. Koefoed, *The Lost Leonardo*, 37:46.
12. Koefoed, *The Lost Leonardo*, 56:05.

of the art agent, Sandy Heller, they enlisted the help of a major auction house, spearheaded by a young man with a unique vision for the painting.[13] This auction of the *Salvator Mundi* would eventually go on to become the most controversial art sale of all time.

13. Vitkine, *Savior for Sale*, 57:32.

Chapter 16: The Oligarch

Dmitry Rybolovlev is a Russian oligarch worth billions of dollars. Initially a medical doctor, he would instead pivot to establishing factories with his father, who was also a doctor. From there, he obtained a brokerage license and set up an investment firm that bought up shares of various businesses, like Uralkali, a company that produces fertilizer. Rybolovlev made billions of dollars from these ventures.[1] The brilliant mindset he carried was in buying these shares at a relatively low price. He seized on opportunities that he knew would be fruitful. This worked so well because many investors have their eyes set on the oil industry and tended to disregard other ventures that did not come with a high price tag. The oligarch was able to buy cheap shares and then watched their value continue to climb. This was done in the early 1990s when Russia was still healing from the economic fallout from the collapse of the Soviet Union.

Russian oligarchs are wealthy business owners who accumulated their wealth during the aftermath of the Soviet Union. Under communist rule, the State owns everything. However, since the Soviet Union had fallen, these assets needed to be offloaded to citizens. So, what ended up happening was private bidders ate up what was available, and often bought them through corrupt means. These entrepreneurs were able to find areas that would bring them wealth, and some of these main areas were in oil, mining, and agriculture. To help with this inequity, the Russian

1. Fedorin, "Dmitry Rybolovlev," line 3.

government looked to open up shares of these businesses so that the average citizen could purchase stocks, rather than only wealthy businessmen. What instead ended up happening was a minority of well-connected people were able to essentially buy all these shares. Little was left for the average person. In 2011, there was a recorded 101 billionaires in Russia.[2] And while Russian oligarchs own much of Russian businesses, the old ways of the communist Soviet Union still live on there. Political activists regularly accuse the Russian government of using these oligarchs as pawns for their own causes.

Seeing that there was minimal competition not only from similar businesses, but also from other investors, Rybolovlev put much of his effort into Uralkali. His investment and energy put into this company was seen as a leading example of how Russia was able to climb out of its economic despair and start becoming a world power. The industry of mineral fertilizers was now seen by governments as an essential asset, and then other investors began to buy up their own shares of these companies due to the demand it had accrued. In June 2010, Rybolovlev sold 53% of his shares to several individuals. The total amount sold cannot be confirmed; however, economists believe it to be in the realm of $5.3 billion. Then in December 2010, Uralkali bought a 20% stake in another fertilizer company that the oligarch had shares in, Silvinit, for $1.4 billion. This ultimately led to the merger of Silvinit and Uralkali the following year.[3] Dmitry Rybolovlev then moved to Monaco, where he would acquire the majority ownership of the professional soccer club AS Monaco.[4]

I do not know Dmitry Rybolovlev, so I cannot say why he moved to Monaco. But people move, and they move often. Certainly, there were big enough motivations for him to make the call to uproot his homebase to a tiny city-state near France and Italy. What I can speak to is the instability of Eastern Europe, and Russia specifically. As of 2023, the Russian border is roughly three times the length of the United States border, and Russia's population

2. Hyatt, "What is an Oligarch?" line 11.

3. Els, "Two Billionaires," lines 8–16.

4. Conn, "Money and Ambition," line 3.

is less than 50% of the United States population. In addition to this existential vulnerability, Russia is on the verge of a population collapse, or in other words, not enough people are having babies to replace their existing population. While the US is also struggling with their own decline in population, they are not open to the same types of exposed dangers as Russia is. So, who really knows the exact reason why the oligarch left his motherland. But a billionaire businessman in Western Europe, to me at least, looks much more promising than being one in the former Soviet Union. Afterall, Monaco is a well-known destination for the world's richest and most powerful people to convene.

Over the years he amassed a very impressive art collection that included a wide range of artists from Paul Gauguin to Mark Rothko. Throughout his years of collecting art, he eventually ended up doing business with Yves Bouvier. Bouvier sold him many works of art at a much higher price than what Rybolovlev initially thought. Reports began to come out about this complex business scheme that suggested Bouvier had scammed him out of about $1 billion. This ordeal is now known as the *Bouvier Affair*.[5] One of the many unfortunate aspects of this is that some of the Picasso paintings he bought that were mediated by Yves Bouvier, were stolen. Rybolovlev returned the paintings.[6] The main reason why scandals like this can take place is that there is no oversight for the sale of high-priced works of art. If you buy a home, then there are multiple entities involved, and pages upon pages of legal paperwork to go along with it. Regarding the sale of artworks, there tends to only be a receipt. It must be granted to Bouvier that he does have a vulpine intelligence about him.

Rybolovlev is a quiet man who avoids the media spotlight. The attention that had turned towards him is something that he has worked his entire professional life to avoid.[7] He has been involved in various controversies over the years, such as his businesses heavily polluting the Kama River in Russia. He was also

5. Koefoed, *The Lost Leonardo*, 39:16.
6. Frank, "Art Scandal Deepens," line 3.
7. Vitkine, *Savior for Sale*, 37:59.

accused of creating a system to illegally buy soccer players' shares, which is known as the *Football Leaks Scandal*. There is always going to be a heavy amount of attention on any Russian oligarch and the financial moves that they make simply because of their wealth status. However, there is no way that the *Bouvier Affair* could just be a minor story. And the oligarch has every intention of going after Bouvier with a rage of vengeance. A businessman who clawed his way out of the mess of the Soviet Union to become a billionaire does not want to be viewed as someone that can be taken advantage of. He has set out to destroy Bouvier in a long, convoluted chain of lawsuits.

The most famous painting in this scandal is the *Salvator Mundi*. Yves Bouvier initially urged caution to Dmitry Rybolovlev about the painting, saying it had a controversial authorship and that there is heavy restoration to the artwork. However, Rybolovlev insisted that he wanted to purchase the work, and instructed Bouvier to make the sale happen. Bouvier negotiated the price of the painting down to eighty million dollars, with an additional three million dollars to the auction house that mediated this sale. However, he told the oligarch that the sale price was $127.5 million, in addition to his commission fee. Rybolovlev agreed to the $127.5 million deal without being aware of the initial purchase price. Bouvier then had the auction house sign a non-disclosure agreement to prevent anyone from knowing, or speaking, about the transaction. The auction house did not conspire with Bouvier but was acting more so as the unknowing middleman for him to flip the painting. Bouvier maintains that this is a common business practice and that there is nothing wrong with selling objects for high prices.[8]

On March 9, 2014, New York Times journalist, Scott Reyburn, got wind of the sale by Yves Bouvier and wrote an article about it. Reyburn did not know at the time that Bouvier had bought the painting for Rybolovlev, and that he was selling it to him at a high markup. Once the oligarch found out what had happened, he would lead a crusade against Bouvier. But instead of immediately

8. Koefoed, *The Lost Leonardo*, 59:31.

going after Bouvier, he decided to lay out a trap for him. Rybo-lovlev invited Bouvier to his home in Monaco, and once Bouvier entered, he was arrested on charges of money laundering. After this initial arrest, a wave of lawsuits from Rybolovlev followed that carried the charge of defalcation against Bouvier.[9] In addition to this, other former art clients of Bouvier unleashed their own lawsuits against him with similar claims of fraud.[10] Bouvier has maintained his innocence throughout these proceedings by essentially saying he can sell his own property for whatever price he sees fit. A major area that has helped him make his case is that there is minimal oversight for sales in the art world. The lawsuits by Bouvier are still ongoing. It is a messy ordeal, and it can be hard to tell if Bouvier was in the wrong. He argues that he can sell his possessions for whatever value he wants. While the oligarch claims ethical breaches.

The oligarch began to see the *Salvator Mundi* as an example of a major mistake he made by choosing to do business with Bouvier. He wanted the painting gone. However, dropping $127.5 million on a painting means that he would want to recoup at least some of that money. The *Salvator Mundi* had already been in the public eye for years now, and only a few people seemed to be that thrilled by the work. Was Rybolovlev just going to have to deal with this financial loss, and focus on selling the other artworks in his possession? Well, no. People were not excited about this painting because it is just not that good of a piece of art. There were also big questions about its attribution. Rybolovlev needed an art expert he could trust with this work, and who could rebrand it as something new, something final. This is when the oligarch put his trust into Christie's Auction House with the hopes of them pulling off something for the history books.

9. Koefoed, *The Lost Leonardo*, 57:33.
10. Mulholland, "Alleged Victims," line 2.

Chapter 17: Lights, Camera, Action

In November 2022, Christie's Auction House anticipated putting a full-scale Tyrannosaurus rex up for auction. This massive dinosaur skeleton was expected to sell for around fifteen and twenty-five million dollars, and bidders were already lining up. However, that same month the auction house pulled the T. Rex from the auction due to authenticity issues. The exact reason for the cancellation was that there were quite a few *bones* in the skeleton that were casts and not the real thing. To be clear, the T. Rex skeleton did contain many of the original bones, it just also contained a good deal of casts.[1] This was a good move on the part of Christie's as they knew that they could not auction off the skeleton in the state that they originally had wanted to. So, if Christie's pulled a dinosaur skeleton because there were too many casts instead of bones, then why would Christie's auction off the *Salvator Mundi* with all its attribution and provenance issues? Maybe because $450.3 million is significantly more than fifteen to twenty-five million. At least the T. Rex contained real bones.

I think there are really two types of nostalgia. One being the warm memories you have with family from a particular time in life that was carefree and full of love. Maybe it was playing at the arcade with your dad or listening to Christmas carolers at a tree lighting celebration. The second type of nostalgia is brand-based. Examples could include a popular toy you played with after a company successfully marketed it to you and your parents. Or maybe

---

1. Jacobs, "Christies Pulls T. Rex," line 3.

it was watching a particular childhood movie that was released with aggressive business partnerships to aid in its promotion. I do not mean to suggest that the brand-based nostalgia is inherently wrong. What I am only wanting to suggest is that we have strong emotional connections to things, and sometimes it is based purely on the experience, and sometimes it is choreographed by external factors. Much of the art market is fueled by external factors.

The reliance on constructing a background to pieces of art is a proven strategy that galleries have used for years. This is a way to build an emotional attachment to a particular work that otherwise would not have been there for the buyer. Someone with an untrained eye for art, or maybe someone who is just beginning the process of collecting, can easily lean too heavily on the backstory of the artist. Gallery assistants will drone on and on about the trials and tribulations the artist had to endure in their life, and then give an overly exhaustive description and meaning of the work. This method can quickly turn a subpar, unsold painting into a subpar painting that has been sold for way more than what it is actually worth. The more someone is around the selling of art then the more they are able to see through this. But there are always fresh collectors who come along with money to burn. In many ways it is at least more honest when art dealers present an artwork as a worthwhile monetary investment. Auction houses help to steer the art market and keep the system open on monetary transparency regarding the price of artworks. Sotheby's and Christie's had both featured my artwork on their Instagram stories in 2020, and that alone helped to increase my art sales.

Auction houses play into the human feeling of both allure and investment. They are the brand-based nostalgia, the gatekeepers of cost, and the standard of what is worth collecting. They are also necessary. Galleries can be selective with whom they sell to, while auction houses dole the product out to whomever is the highest bidder. Art selling in a major auction is a transparent way to find out the cost of the work. Without auction houses then that would leave us with private sales, and gallery transactions. And if you have ever been to a high-end art gallery, you are quick to note that prices can never be found. Auction houses show us in real time the exact price an artwork sells for. The full transparency is needed, even if the sale price of some of the artworks make your stomach churn. If the Holy Trinity of the Renaissance is Leonardo da Vinci, Michelangelo, and Raphael, then the Holy Trinity of auction houses are Phillips, Christie's, and Sotheby's. And Christie's won the bid to sell the *Salvator Mundi*.

Dmitry Rybolovlev enlisted Christie's Auction House to take on the challenge of selling this painting. Christie's needed to ensure the best person from their lineup would lead the charge for the sale. This would be Loic Gouzer, who was still only in his thirties. Gouzer would lead a strong marketing campaign that involved a brilliant promotional video. This video showed people of all ages staring at the *Salvator Mundi*. However, we only see the people's faces in this video, and never the actual work. This type of marketing is one that provided the emotional intensity attributed to the power of this painting. Even the actor Leonardo DiCaprio was one of the people shown in the video. Gouzer and DiCaprio are friendly with one another and have worked together on fundraising campaigns for various charities.[2] There seemed to be one straightforward goal with the marketing, and that was to persuade people into thinking this mediocre artwork was not only painted by Leonardo, but that it was the best painting he had ever done. It would not take long for it to start being referred to as *The Last Leonardo*.

Christie's sent the artwork on a worldwide tour to help with the promotion of the painting. Swarms of people waited in long lines to get their chance to see the painting in the flesh. Gouzer knew that he couldn't just speak about the painting for it to gain mythical status, it needed to be in front of as many people as possible who would talk about it. And all of those people have phones, which they then started broadcasting on social media platforms. Before long, the hype of the *Salvator Mundi* had erupted like a volcano, drowning out the art scholars who questioned the legitimacy of its authorship. If massive crowds were willing to patiently

2. Neuendorf, "Meteoric Career," line 7.

wait in line to see this artwork, then the thousands of posts about it on social media would catapult this artwork into mythical status. The painting was taken to Hong Kong, London, San Francisco, and New York in 2017. Each location produced great turnouts and was very popular among those who saw it. Christie's also suggested that Carmen Bambach attributed this painting to da Vinci. She, however, stated she never attributed the painting to him, and re-iterated that she believes his student, Boltraffio, is most likely the author of the work.[3]

Now the painting was finally ready for the big time. Christie's produced a 162-page book on the *Salvator Mundi*, quoting people who have nothing to do with the painting itself, like the Russian novelist Fyodor Dostoevsky, and the neurologist Sigmund Freud. Christie's used quotes by great thinkers and put them in the book to give off more of the appearance that this painting was something special. Another brilliant move by Gouzer was that he placed it within their Contemporary Auction Sale, and not an Old Masters Sale.[4] Other than placing it in this type of auction for publicity, why would it be put up this way? Because the majority of the painting was done by Dianne Modestini. The *Salvator Mundi* was truly a work of contemporary art, not of a historical one. Certainly, the original painting was executed around 1500 and probably did come straight out of Leonardo da Vinci's workshop. But it was not painted by him. It was most likely done by a student. And whichever student did do this painting, very little of the original paint was still on the canvas. This left the restorer, Modestini, to fill in the many gaps.

The auction took place on the evening of November 15th, 2017, and took only minutes to complete, with an opening bid of $100 million. The price went to $140, $150, and then jumped to $300 million after a few minutes, then $350. After this price announcement, the room went quiet for a moment. Then a bid for $352 million came in, which made the audience chuckle as that was such a miniscule increment when compared to the overall

3. Vitkine, *Savior for Sale*, 1:21:35.

4. Vitkine, *Savior for Sale*, 1:00:02.

price that was already willing to be paid. Then came $355 million, then $370 million to a relatively quiet room at this point. Shortly after came the $400 million bid. The people in the audience immediately, and loudly, gasped followed by applause. This was the winning bid, $400 million. This resulted in a grand total of $450,312,500, when including the auction house fees, for the *Salvator Mundi*. Everyone in the room had their phones out recording this moment. When the hammer price fell, they all roared with cheers. Gouzer was able to take a bad painting, with a bad provenance and attribution issues, and sell it for nearly half a billion dollars. The most scandalous art sale of all time.

In December 2018, Gouzer announced that he was stepping down from Christie's Auction House, saying that he intended to focus on conservation and climate issues.[5] He emerged a couple years later with other art ventures, only this time they would not be involved with auction houses. A few months before the infamous auction, the restorer of the *Salvator Mundi*, Dianne Modestini, was presented an honorary doctorate of Humane Letters by Fairfield University. This is in addition to the undisclosed sum she was given by Parish and Simon after they had sold the work to Yves Bouvier. So, at the end of the day, everyone gets paid. In addition, auction records are set, doctorate degrees are given, and early retirement becomes more of a possibility. But the one that paid all this money for the artwork is the one left holding the hot potato. It would not take too long for reports to start coming out that Saudi Arabian Prince Badr bin Abdullah bought it on behalf of Saudi Arabian Crown Prince, Mohammed bin Salman Al Saud. The painting was thought to be going to the Louvre's outpost museum in Abu Dhabi. However, the *Salvator Mundi* never made its way to the museum, and would instead go missing.

5. Pogrebin, "Rule-Breaking Rainmaker," line 1.

Chapter 18: Princely Things

In early October 2018, less than a year after the infamous auction of the *Salvator Mundi,* Jamal Khashoggi entered a Saudi consulate in Istanbul, Turkey and would not leave the building alive. A dual investigation between the Turkish and Saudi governments took place and Saudi Arabia's original stance on the matter was to deny that he was murdered. Later, the Saudi government acknowledged his death, and the following month the United States Central Intelligence Agency claimed that Khashoggi was assassinated under direct orders from Crown Prince Mohammad bin Salman, aka MBS.[1] The news of this murder plot sent shock waves around the world and added to political tensions, particularly between the US and Saudi Arabia. Khashoggi was murdered and his body cut up into pieces, stuffed into bags, and transported out of the government building. He left behind four children and a fiancée. He was fifty-nine years old.

Jamal Khashoggi was a journalist and outspoken critic of the Saudi Arabian regime, and he came from a prominent family. His uncle, Adnan Khashoggi, was a wealthy arms dealer, and his grandfather, Muhammad Khashoggi, was King Abdulaziz Al Saud's personal doctor. Khashoggi wrote for big name media outlets from The Washington Post to Al Watan, a Saudi newspaper. He was critical of the Saudi Royal family, outspoken against their war in Yemen, was a proponent of freedom of expression, against strict Wahhabi laws, and many other things. He was a thorn in

---

1. Fogel, *Dissident,* 1:40:54.

- and that his nation needs to have other areas of making money. Re-newable energy is a popular venture for many countries and MBSannounced that they would be investing $100 billion into variousrenewable energy projects. They also set a goal to have 50% of theirelectricity come from renewable energy by 2030. Saudi Arabia also

Selling Leonardo

the side of the Saudi government. In September 2019, MBS again
said that he did not give order for the murder of Khashoggi, but
that he bears the responsibility for the death due to being a main
leader of Saudi Arabia.[2] That same year in December, Saudi courts
sentenced five people to death, and three other people to prison
for twenty-four year sentences each. The entire trial was done in
secrecy, including the concealment of all evidence and names of
the accused from the public. In May 2020, during the Islamic holy
month of Ramadan, Khashoggi's children publicly forgave the
five people sentenced to death. Under Saudi law, this commutes
their sentence away from the death penalty.[3] The pardoning of the
people found guilty of premeditated murder raises even more red
flags as to why this decision by his family was made.

The assassination of Khashoggi was a setback for MBS and
his vision for Saudi Arabia. MBS sees oil production as a critical
asset to the country but is also aware of this being a finite resource,
and that his nation needs to have other areas of making money. Renewable energy is a popular venture for many countries and MBS
has looked to enter this territory as well. In 2022, Saudi Arabia
announced that they would be investing $100 billion into various
renewable energy projects. They also set a goal to have 50% of their
electricity come from renewable energy by 2030. Saudi Arabia also
announced plans to develop a dystopian city that they call *The
Line*, which is essentially a thin city in between reflective walls.
This city is to stretch more than 105 miles long, be 220 yards wide,
and more than 540 yards high, and is to house 1.5 million people
by 2030 while running solely on renewable energy.[4] This apoca-
lyptic government housing solution is the strange, authoritarian
vision that MBS has for the people who live under his rule. Renewable energy, housing inside a wall, and butchered journalists.

Saudi Arabia operates under Sharia Law, and this has led to
blatant discrimination against people of various religions, including against people without a religion. The Mutawa is a religious

2. Graham, "Saudi Crown Prince," lines 1–4.
3. Tawfeeq, "Sparing Them," lines 1–3.
4. Bantock, "Future or Fantasy?," lines 1–6.

100

police force that functions within the borders of Saudi Arabia. Their main job is to maintain the separation of the sexes in public, prevent people from conducting business during prayer times, and enforce strict traditional dress wear. An infamous case involving the Mutawa was in 2002 when a school caught fire in Mecca. Fifteen schoolgirls burned to death because the Mutawa would not allow any male rescuers inside the building as the girls were not veiled. Horrific stories such as this one poses a threat to MBS and what he sees for the future of Saudi Arabia. He knows that his country cannot remain isolated and that our global economy creates a mounting pressure. The United Arab Emirates, UAE, which borders Saudi Arabia has successfully established cities such as Abu Dhabi and Dubai as vacation destinations. They are also places for wealthy businessmen to travel to with their families. This is not happening in Saudi Arabia. MBS knows that he must take steps towards opening his country without also losing his grip on the land.

MBS would take some minor steps in making Saudi Arabia more digestible for the Western world, such as in 2018 when women were allowed to drive motor vehicles. He also set his sights on art, knowing that this is an easy way to build a bridge between cultures. During the Renaissance, the Medici family was quite successful in obtaining allies via arts and culture too. The question that remains in the air is if Saudi Arabia can pull of something similar. In recent years there has been a major uptick in art fairs and festivals in Saudi Arabia. From temporary to permanent art installations, to art galleries and museums, MBS has been overseeing all of this. One of these exhibits is Desert X AlUla, which showcases both Saudi and international artists' work in the desert. These installations have received high praise from art critics and shows the rest of the world that Saudi Arabia can compete with the other major players of the contemporary art scene. All of this has occurred in a relatively quick time frame. The arts are being pushed heavily by the Saudi regime to modernize themselves, and to not give off the appearance of running a brutal, oppressive regime. Art can often hide things like this.

And sports

It comes as no surprise that MBS would pay $450.3 million for the *Salvator Mundi*. The speculation as to why he would spend this kind of money on a bad painting, with terrible provenance, and big attribution issues, suddenly becomes clearer for two reasons. The first reason being that $450.3 million is of no issue to House of Saud. And secondly, even with all the problems associated with the painting, it is a way to get all eyes on Saudi Arabia. This can help to legitimize moves they are making in order to function in a modernized world. Art is a crucial piece, but still just one piece to his equation. With the sale of the *Salvator Mundi*, the rest of the world is now talking about Saudi Arabia in a context other than the oil business and their human rights violations. Fake or not, buying the most expensive painting ever sold gets people to view Saudi Arabia in a different light. And when this painting does go up to be displayed, the world will once again be talking about Saudi Arabia in the context of art. To this regime, it doesn't really matter who painted the work, but rather how many people are going to be talking about it.

Stefan Simchowitz is a notorious and well-respected art dealer that I have had many friendly conversations with. When I asked about his opinion on the matter he told me, with permission to publicly share, "A painting whose apotheosis becomes a symbolic 21st Century vessel that represents the shifting powers from West to East. The work, and I mean the work as it is attached to the event surrounding the work, are functionally one and the same, inseparable at this point. It becomes the symbol of power transfer politically, economically, and socially. Jesus is back home." The world operates on oil. Regardless of someone's stance on the environment and renewable energy, at this present moment, a society without oil is a society that collapses. Saudi Arabia has been brilliantly strategic with their use of this finite resource and have been able to establish a powerful empire because of it. But without strong, reliable allies, then being the hoarder of a natural resource can only carry them so far. The purchase of the *Salvator Mundi* shows the world that they are more than a Wahhabi society with a ton of oil. Art on its own tends to only matter on an individual level; such as if someone enjoys the work or not. But on a global scale, art is a way to show that a society is ready to open up to the rest of the world.

But just as MBS was starting to gain international favor for the arts, with much help from the purchase of the *Salvator Mundi*, Khashoggi's assassination left a sour taste in people's mouths. This coordinated murder of the famed journalist led a ripple effect of powerful players in the art world to no longer associate with Saudi Arabia. Tad Smith, the CEO of Sotheby's, pulled out of an economic conference that was to be hosted by MBS. Several museums cut ties with the Saudi Kingdom. A Washington D.C. based think-tank, the Middle East Institute, in which Khashoggi was a regular collaborator, pulled their support from the Arab Art & Education Initiative. In addition, the Metropolitan Museum and Brooklyn Museum refused Saudi funding for upcoming exhibitions and seminars. Other institutions, such as Columbia University, with ties to Saudi money also announced that they would refuse to accept funds from them.[5] The list continues on with other foundations that either temporarily, or permanently refused to collaborate with Saudi Royalty. Trouble would also mount when it came to light that Saudi Arabia had recruited Twitter employees to spy on Saudi dissidents and report their findings to the Royal Family. One of these spies was convicted by a US grand jury in 2022.[6] The public relations nightmare was a major setback for the Crown Prince.

Jeff Bezos, the billionaire founder of Amazon, was friendly with MBS and was planning business investments in Saudi Arabia. However, after the murder of Khashoggi, Bezos ceased contact with MBS. Bezos has several business ventures other than just Amazon, he is also the owner of The Washington Post newspaper, for whom Khashoggi was a journalist. The Washington Post ran a massive campaign called, *Justice for Jamal*, which put enormous pressure on MBS. Bezos allowed this journalistic campaign to continue in order to show support for Jamal Khashoggi. Shortly after the business relationship between MBS and Bezos had soured,

5. Weber, "Major Art Institutions," lines 2–7.
6. Stempel, "Twitter Employee," line 1.

Bezos' phone was then hacked with Pegasus spyware. Intelligence agencies in coordination with the United Nations confirmed that Pegasus infiltrated Bezos' phone through a text message sent to him by Saudi Arabia. It was also around this time the National Enquirer was running stories about Bezos saying that they had secret information he had been having a marital affair. Further, there was a massive social media campaign run by Saudi nationals that directly targeted Jeff Bezos.[7] MBS has a desire to bring Saudi Arabia to the forefront as world leaders, but allegations such as this are major setbacks.

After MBS acquired the *Salvator Mundi*, the painting essentially disappeared. No one knew where it was, and Saudi officials would not make any public comments regarding its whereabouts. However, reports started to come out saying that it would go on loan to the Louvre for an exhibit celebrating the 500th anniversary of Leonardo da Vinci's death. The exhibition would showcase several of da Vinci's paintings, as well as twenty-two drawings of his. These reports started to become more and more credible as it came closer to the opening date, and many insiders believed this would now be the grand reappearance of the painting. But it never showed. Rumors began to run rampant as to the reasoning behind this. But the Louvre carried on with their exhibition, only without the *Salvator Mundi*. The Louvre Abu Dhabi was another museum that was expected to receive the painting as a loan, but it never showed there either.[8] There quickly became a growing worry about the delicate nature of the painting because of its age. If the painting was not in a museum, and no one knew where it was, then the fear of it never appearing in public again could become a permanent reality.

7. Fogel, *Dissident*, 1:37:34.

8. Vitkine, *Savior for Sale*, 1:24:50.

Chapter 19: The Palace

In addition to going inside the Louvre, it is also worthwhile to spend time outside of it. The Cour Napoleon, the courtyard hugged between the two arms of the building, is filled with great statues on the outside of it. Erin and I set out to find the Arago medallion located on the grounds of the courtyard. Just as I was complaining to her that we could not find this seemingly impossible medallion, she spotted it right underneath my feet. There are 135 of these bronze markers laid into the ground. They create a straight line through the city from Porte de Clignancourt in the north, to Gentilly in the south. The Arago medallions represent the Paris Meridian, and one of them is in the Cour Napoleon at the Louvre. In this courtyard also lies the several glass pyramids designed by the Chinese-American architect I. M. Pei, completed in 1988. These beautiful glass pyramids help to illuminate the Louvre and marry the present to the past.

Erin had fallen in love with the Louvre from the moment we first walked through its courtyard. She was truly awestruck by the magnificence of both the building and the artworks and artifacts it holds. A few weeks after we had returned to the United States, the Louvre publicly announced that they were attempting to obtain an artwork known as the *Duc de Choiseul Snuffbox*. This small artifact is only 8 cm long, 6 cm wide, and 2.5 cm high. It was created between 1770 and 1771 for François de Choiseul, a high-ranking military officer who was also the Chief Minister of France. Louis Roucel beautifully adorned gold around the snuffbox, and the box was intricately painted by the French artist, Louis-Nicolas van

Blarenberghe. Coming from a family of artists, Blarenberghe was well-respected in the French courts and received many commissions. While we do not know the identity of who exactly commissioned the snuffbox, it does depict Choiseul at the height of his government career, right before his fall from favor. Choiseul would mobilize French troops in preparation for a war over the Falkland Islands, something that King Louis XV strongly opposed, which ultimately led to Choiseul losing his position and being banned from government leadership. The snuffbox depicts six different painted scenes of Choiseul in various modes of his high-profile life, including a scene that Blarenberghe painted that shows the Louvre before it was a museum. This part of the snuffbox is the only visual record we have of the original decoration of the *Grande Galerie* in the Louvre.[1]

Inspired by both the story of the snuffbox and her recent time spent at the Louvre, Erin coordinated with the museum and donated money to help them acquire this artwork for their permanent collection. Her efforts with this acquisition earned her a *Thank You Letter* and an official certificate from the museum for playing a role in bringing the *Duc de Choiseul Snuffbox* to the Louvre's collection. The Louvre also invited her to attend private viewings in their museum because of the work that she had done. Her talented eye for the arts, as well as a willingness to take part in it, has led her to now have her name forever documented with the Louvre Museum. There are so many ways to take part in the art world, but if you put the necessary time and energy into it, you can become a major player. The walls built up around the art world are imaginary. People with the right talents for the right projects are the ones who will always get to play a role. One of the impressive ways Erin has been able to find her own role in the art world is through moments such as helping the Louvre acquire the *Duc de Choiseul Snuffbox*. Her name will always remain in the Louvre because of her assistance with helping them obtain this artwork, which now lives in a palace with a grand history.

1. Bloomquist, "The Choiseul Box," 53.

The Louvre dates all the way back to the 12th century where its foundation was built under orders from King Philip II for protection from the Kingdom of England. Parts of the Louvre from this Medieval period still exist in the museum's crypt.[2] Later on in 1682, King Louis XIV moved the royal residence to the Palace at Versailles. This move prompted the Louvre to then begin collecting works of art. After the overthrow of the French monarchy, the Louvre opened its doors as a public museum in 1793, displaying more than seven hundred works of art. The Louvre was quickly becoming recognized as more than just another museum. Its collection grew so rapidly that it had to temporarily close its doors from 1796 to 1801 for necessary updates and repairs. Under the leadership of Napoleon Bonaparte, the collection continued to grow immensely and was able to amass thousands of artworks. A key figure who partnered with Napoleon was the museum's first decorator, Dominique Vivant Denon, who helped steer the vision of the palace. In fact, the most popular wing of the Louvre Museum is named after Denon, and deservedly so as he was well-known for his great eye for art.[3] This wing of the museum is home to all of the da Vinci paintings in its collection and gets crowded very quickly for apparent reasons.

The Louvre is the most visited museum in the world. Located in Paris, and having a collection of well over 480,000 works, contributes to the huge number of visitors every year. It also houses the largest cache of works by Leonardo da Vinci. So, if there is a newly discovered painting by da Vinci, then it can be reasonable to think that the Louvre would at least be able to show it for a time. This is also a great way for MBS to help begin rebuilding trust with other governments. Practicing cultural diplomacy, just as the Medici family in Florence did, could be seen as extending an olive branch that could lead to other financially motivated endeavors. In fact, if MBS was fully confident in the attribution of the *Salvator Mundi*, then he could have paraded the painting around the globe before placing it on display in his home country. However,

2. Edwards, *Old and New*, 193.

3. Nowinski, *Hedonist and Scholar*, 24.

too many people, including da Vinci scholars, do not carry a favorable view of the work. Perhaps simply putting the painting on loan would be enough and could help shift the focus of Saudi Arabia to more cosmopolitan matters like the arts. The matter also ultimately becomes clear when taking into consideration the fact that MBS and the Saudi regime are looking to be a force that is not limited to oil production. Branching out in ways so that they are not viewed by the rest of the world as a hostile nation is beneficial. But the loan would never happen.

The Louvre had every expectation of MBS loaning the *Salvator Mundi* to them for their 500th Anniversary exhibition of Leonardo's work. We know this because they wrote a catalogue book about the painting in case they were able to put the painting on display in their museum. This catalogue was even briefly put up for sale at their gift shop before quickly being pulled off the shelves.[4] When the existence of this catalogue was made known to the public, it could not be found anywhere for purchase. Some conspiratorial thinking arose as to why the Louvre would essentially create and then destroy a book they published. The reasoning behind this is much simpler because the Louvre cannot publicly authenticate or give professional opinions, in any form, for an artwork not within either their temporary or permanent collection. So, since the *Salvator Mundi* never made it to the Leonardo exhibit, the Louvre would not have this book for sale. There still remains the question of what was included within this book, and fortunately a few people were able to get their hands on it before it was pulled.

Before the material within this book was made public, I heard rumors that the museum did not fully attribute the painting to Leonardo da Vinci. This reinvigorated those who did not believe the given authorship of the painting because they now had the Louvre in their corner to help their case. This short, forty-five-page book simply titled, "Leonardo da Vinci: The *Salvator Mundi*", comes down on the side of saying that it *seems* like it could have been painted by Leonardo. The main reasons as to why they are of this opinion is because of the powdered glass used in the priming,

4. Koefoed, *The Lost Leonardo*, 1:28:35.

and the use of vermilion in the shadows and hair.[5] To humbly push back on the Louvre regarding this last point, vermilion was commonly used by Old Masters and their students, particularly for tasks such as painting hair and shadows. Dianne Modestini even chimed in regarding this book saying that there is nothing about the Louvre's findings that she herself did not already know. Modestini has been publicly publishing what she found during her time with the *Salvator Mundi* and speaking about it openly. So, while this book creates an exciting headline, it does not seem to reveal any knowledge about the artwork that was not already available. And the last point regarding this is that it is not clear how the Louvre would have attributed the painting. According to what was in the book, they could have listed the painting as fully, or partially attributed to Leonardo da Vinci. But since the painting never got the chance to be shown there, we will never know.

But why did the Saudis end up refusing to loan the *Salvator Mundi* for the Louvre's grand Leonardo exhibition? Because MBS wanted the Louvre to display the *Salvator Mundi* right next to the *Mona Lisa*. No excuses, no compromising, and certainly no questions. The Louvre refused.[6] If any painting were to be presented next to the *Mona Lisa*, then it would quite literally put that painting on the same pedestal as the greatest artwork to ever exist. So, if the *Salvator Mundi* was put up next to the *Mona Lisa*, and thousands of people came to view it, then MBS could take this painting back to Saudi Arabia claiming it as the male equivalent. Curatorial decisions matter, and MBS knows this. But since the Louvre refused to give in to MBS's demand, they never received the *Salvator Mundi*, and the book that they published had to be removed from the shelves. There is enough speculation remaining here to also wonder if this book was created as a way to give in to Saudi pressure. I have heard speculation that at the beginning of this book, the then-President of the Louvre, Jean-Luc Martinez, wrote that he personally believed the painting to have been made by Leonardo. In May 2022, Martinez was arrested by French police

5. Cole, "Louvre Concealed," line 3.
6. Kelleher, "Pressed the Louvre," lines 9–10.

and charged with money laundering and illegal antiquities trafficking, unrelated to the *Salvator Mundi*.[7]

7. Berger, "Louvre President Charged," lines 1–2.

Chapter 20: Knock-Off Version

A t the time of this writing, reports are circulating that the charges against Jean Luc Martinez may be dropped.[1] Working in the art world is nothing if not convoluted, and the Louvre has many areas of concern. The United Arab Emirates, UAE, lies on the eastern end of the Arabian Peninsula, bordering Saudi Arabia. There are seven *emirates,* each governed by their own emir, and they collectively form the Federal Supreme Council. This Council is then used to elect their President and Vice President. The main export, and overall financial gains, for the UAE comes from petroleum and natural gas. Billions of dollars from these natural resources alone have helped to sustain the UAE's economic power. With the nation's embrace of Sharia Law, there have been many claims of human rights abuses. Apostasy is punishable by death, rape victims themselves have been imprisoned, and human rights activists have been jailed and tortured for speaking out. In contrast, the UAE also relies on tourism. Dubai and Abu Dhabi are popular travel destinations that have provided a way for the UAE to try to bring themselves into the modern world. Their attempt at balancing outdated laws, while competing with Western entertainment, has shown this strange irony.

In addition to the production of petroleum and natural gas, and tourism, the UAE has looked for other ways to expand their economic strength. In 2017, the same year that the *Salvator Mundi* was sold at auction, the UAE hosted the FIFA Club World Cup for

---

1. Noce, "Antiquity Charges," line 1.

111

soccer. This would help popularize the UAE even more and put them on a global stage. Another way that the UAE has looked to modernize their nation is through art. After all, art is cross cultural, and can bring in substantial revenue. The many oil magnates and other businesspeople from around the world coming there have money to spend. Art galleries, auctions, and museums are all areas that can help bring in additional revenue. This happens while simultaneously helping the UAE to refashion itself as a contemporary ally bridging the gap between the East and the West. In order for countries to compete as a world power, there need to be elements of sophistication to them. Opening up the country for tourism and major sporting events is a great start, and art is a natural component to be added to the equation.

In 2007, the UAE and France signed an agreement that would allow the Middle Eastern nation to use the Louvre name for one of their own museums. This agreement was written to last until the year 2037, with the option for the UAE to renew the contract to continue their use of the name. Discussions between the two countries for this business deal began in 2005, so only a two-year turnaround seems to suggest that France was eager for this contract to take effect. The UAE paid France four hundred million dollars for the rights to use the Louvre name, but they would pay up much more than just that. In addition to the four hundred million dollars, they coughed up $190 million for art loans, seventy-five million for exhibitions, $165 million for advice from the Louvre staff in Paris, and another twenty-five million dollars for the UAE to have the right to name an area inside the Louvre Museum in Paris after Zayed bin Sultan Al Nahyan, a founding father of the UAE.[2] This means that the UAE paid close to one billion dollars to France, just to use the Louvre's name and receive support from them. In other words, the Louvre Abu Dhabi is no *Louvre* at all. It is just a museum that paid almost a billion dollars to borrow the name of the world's most famous museum. It is all a façade.

With MBS looking to modernize his own nation and strengthen alliances with the countries that border his, having

2. Riding, "Louvre's Name: Expensive," lines 5–12.

cultural exchanges is a method that usually works. Countries that share their culture and heritage with one another share a bond between them, which can make it less likely for tensions to arise. Shortly after it was known that MBS was the purchaser of the *Salvator Mundi*, reports began circulating that the painting would be loaned to the Louvre Abu Dhabi. The word began to spread that the most expensive painting in the world would be on a public viewing in the Middle East. The UAE carries a lot of wealth, and a ton of wealthy businessmen travel to the UAE for work. Opening the Louvre Abu Dhabi that displays what was thought to be an authentic Leonardo da Vinci, would be more reason for these businessmen to bring their family and friends along. Speculation regarding the painting's authenticity began to grow rampant after the auction. No longer was this just some painting that a few scholars believed to be the real deal. Now all eyes were on it, and the argument against its given authorship had grown. During this time, the Louvre Abu Dhabi received notification that they would no longer be receiving the painting as a loan. The museum was also not informed of its whereabouts.

The fallout MBS had with the actual Louvre, and now the fake Louvre in Abu Dhabi, only added oil to the fire that was already burning around this painting. MBS remained quiet during this whole process, and the Saudi government in general would be quiet too. Rumors grew, and no one knew where the painting was. Credible sources believed that MBS kept the *Salvator Mundi* on his 440-foot yacht named the *Serene*. This yacht cost the Saudi Prince a cool six-hundred million dollars.[3] So, with just the yacht and the painting aboard the ship, there was over one billion dollars floating on top of the sea. I spoke with art conservationists who expressed outrage to me when they heard a painting as old as this one was aboard a yacht. Seawater can cause significant damage to it. Paintings are delicate in nature, and the chemical process of dried paint on the canvas requires ideal conditions for it to maintain its desired appearance. Something as little as mists from the seawater can easily infect the paint. An artwork as old

3. Said, Crow, and Faucon, "Saudi Leader's Yacht," line 3.

as this one should really be in a room with ideal temperature and humidity levels.

In October of 2022, reports came out that the *Salvator Mundi* was within the borders of Saudi Arabia, and that the Saudi Crown Prince was constructing a museum precisely for the painting.[4] Little information regarding this museum was made known at the time, such as where in Saudi Arabia it would be located. But what was clear was that MBS now had every intention of keeping that painting inside the nation in which he rules. MBS had even personally invited Martin Kemp to go to their country for a private viewing and inspection of the work. At this point in time, Kemp has remained steadfast in his belief that the work was done by da Vinci. However, when later asked about this request from MBS, Kemp seemed to show hesitation with travelling to Saudi Arabia. He did say that he would do it for the sake of the art.[5] Regardless of the nature of this request, the *Salvator Mundi* will once again be heading towards the spotlight. And just to tidy up this mess, MBS refused to loan the *Salvator Mundi* to the Louvre because they refused to show it next to the *Mona Lisa*. Around this time, the painting was also supposed to be put on loan to the fake Louvre in Abu Dhabi but was pulled last minute. And now MBS is to build the *Salvator Mundi* its own museum in Saudi Arabia. Because if you display a painting within a museum built just for it, then it is much harder for the average art-goer to question its authenticity.

As for the Louvre Abu Dhabi, it remains a popular museum in the UAE, with millions of people having already visited it. France received so much money from the UAE for letting their museum use the Louvre name that it would be reasonable to suggest that this contract could be further extended. The French government is unique in the sense that it oversees every museum in their country. Since this is the case, the French government has been heavily involved with the Louvre Abu Dhabi. This Middle Eastern museum has been able have works of art loaned from other French museums as well, such as the Centre Georges Pompidou and the

4. Cascone, "Special Museum," lines 2–3.
5. Cascone, "Special Museum," lines 6–7.

Musée d'Orsay. I completed my own Copyist work, renditions of the *Mona Lisa* and *Saint John the Baptist*, at the Louvre on September 26th, 2022. On October 18th, 2022, the Louvre announced on social media that da Vinci's painting, *Saint John the Baptist*, was shipped off to the Louvre Abu Dhabi. It will remain on loan at that museum for two full years.

Chapter 21: One Final Discovery

In the winter of 2023, I was viewing various art prints to possibly purchase, and came across an original Jonas Wood print from 2015. The price seemed reasonable for what it was, and I decided to do more research on the work. The dealer told me that he received the artwork from a contact he had in Hong Kong. This is not too much of concern, especially since I was able to easily track down the artist's show during that timeframe. What I also found was the website which displayed this work. It turns out that this *artwork* was not an original print at all. This work that was being sold was actually a picture of a painting Jonas Wood did that was shown in a catalogue, which I located. Inside this catalogue was a high-resolution photograph of the painting spread out across two pages. The *artwork* that this dealer was trying to peddle was of the left-hand side page in the catalogue. This is not a piece of art at all, but rather a photograph of a painting. I further proved my discovery by showing that the image was cutoff at its right side, leaving out the other part of the original work. When comparing the fake art to the actual painting, you can see that there is a whole other portion that is left out of the image and being sold as an authentic print. I reported my findings to the authorities. Trust and knowledge are essential for surviving in the art world.

Art is a tough subject because it cannot be measured. With sports, whoever scores the most points, wins the game. With math, there is no correct answer without a properly completed equation. But art does not cling to these measurements. Some say that art is subjective, but I do not think that is the case either. The more devotion a person has to the arts, then the better their understanding of it becomes. Another aspect with art is that it does not need to serve a utilitarian function. A fork, no matter how beautifully or wretchedly crafted one may be, is meant to help you eat. A chair, regardless of how much skill is involved in its creation, is meant for people to sit on. Art will not fill an empty stomach. It will not purify dirty water. And it will not drive you to work. What art does do is exist, and that is all. Do we need art? Probably not. At least not in the sense for survival. But I do think that is the wrong question to ask. Art has been with us since the beginning. Humans have always had a desire to create images and experiences just for the sake of it. Art will not cure diseases, and art will not keep society safe. What art does do is serve as a reminder that we are human, and it helps us to feel our emotions.

After I completed my renditions of the *Mona Lisa* and *Saint John the Baptist*, Erin and I spent more time in the Louvre. The high ceilings and walls filled with masterpieces made me feel humbled and honored to have painted in their presence. Getting admitted to the Louvre as an official Copyist is highly competitive and requires a great amount of skill and determination to be accepted. Thoughts of imposter syndrome still come to me, and I must remind myself that it was the Louvre itself that selected me. I had worked hard to get the permit, but it is my gratefulness that sometimes morphs into feelings of self-doubt. Being chosen as a Copyist at the Louvre is one of the greatest honors of my life. Prior to painting in the Louvre, my artwork had entered the collection of two separate museums. Both of those times left me with an intense feeling of excitement, and a desire to keep pushing forward. I poured all that I had into creating those paintings in the Louvre. When the paintings were completed, I knew that I had given everything I had to the arts. I took my understanding of Leonardo da Vinci and tried my best to frame his paintings in a contemporary, abstract 2022 context.

The time spent between getting the acceptance letter from the Louvre in June, to completing the paintings there in September, was absorbing as much information as I could. And while preparing,

I always kept in the back of my mind the clues that might link da Vinci to the *Salvator Mundi*. What I walked away with was an even more well-footed stance that he did not create that painting. The subtle tricep of *Saint John the Baptist*, and the winding roads in the *Mona Lisa*, are evidence of work having been created by a highly skilled artist. Da Vinci took great care to construct proper imagery. But the *Salvator Mundi* is an image of a stoned-looking Jesus wearing a tacky harness. It does not equate to the same creator. Remember, the *Salvator Mundi* was made around the same time as both the *Mona Lisa* and *Saint John the Baptist*. There are stunning similarities between those two, and there are notebook sketches of his that help build off these creations. But there are essentially no similarities between those two artworks and the *Salvator Mundi*. Even the drawings of the robes in his notebooks are weak evidence at best. It is difficult to fathom that da Vinci, at the height of his career, would decide to make a subpar painting.

After returning from Paris, I finished up my Copyist renditions with some minor touch ups to properly fill out the image. I felt accomplished and ready to take on more work. In the weeks following, I received a small wave of commissions from art collectors. While I certainly make more money from art than what I put into it, sales are not always consistent. Therefore, it came as a shock to me to have received all these various commissions in a short time frame. Regarding what I see for my own art in the future, the only thing I am certain of is that I will continue making art. The galleries I have signed with and the art I have sold has created a strong foundation for myself. The museums that have collected my artwork has helped to further legitimize myself as an artist. And now being an official Copyist at the Louvre has shown me that my art is somewhere within the art history canon. Yet I know that I will always want more. There will always be a new goal. Being a Copyist at the Louvre is very difficult because they only allow a small number of talented people to participate, and they are incredibly selective. I am forever grateful that they chose me. And I will always carry with me my experience as a Louvre Copyist.

Chapter 21: One Final Discovery

And so, this adventure still leaves us with the status of the *Salvator Mundi*. MBS halted plans to show it at the Louvre after they denied his request to display it next to the *Mona Lisa*. He then refused to show it at the Louvre Abu Dhabi, and recently it now seems that this is because he is having his own museum built for it in Saudi Arabia. The assassination and bodily dismemberment of journalist Jamal Khashoggi in 2018 still carries a dark cloud over the regime. Nevertheless, MBS continues to push forward with plans to make his country more than just a land with oil. An attraction of having not only the world's most expensive painting, but also most controversial painting, seems to be a starting point. In addition to all of this, Saudi Arabia continues to struggle with perceptions of human rights abuses. While it looks like the tide is somewhat turning for them, there are moments where it all seems to be more of a façade than anything else. I had a conversation with artist and art dealer, Kenny Schachter, about MBS and the *Salvator Mundi*, and he shares my concerns on the matter. He said to me, and with permission to share this quote, "The painting was bought as a tourist attraction...Whether or not it's actually by da Vinci is irrelevant- a hair, a finger- it's more distinguishing characteristic is the price tag."

The Russian Oligarch, Dmitry Rybolovlev, paid a little more than $127 million for the *Salvator Mundi*. He then quickly brought it to auction where it sold for the historically high price of $450.3 million, including the auction house fees. Thus, getting him much more of his money back than what Yves Bouvier had gotten from him. The so-called *Bouvier Affair* is still ongoing and does not have any end in sight. It looks as though Rybolovlev will continue his international lawsuits against Bouvier for the rest of his time on earth. And of course, Alexander Parish and Robert Simon, who sold the *Salvator Mundi* to Bouvier for eighty million dollars, floated some of that cash to the restorer, Dianne Modestini.[1] The recipe for this notorious art sale requires little ingredients to make a few people very rich. This includes one subpar painting from Leonardo's workshop. Then you need two out of five art experts

---

1. Koefoed, *The Lost Leonardo*, 37:46.

to secretly give a hesitant approval of attribution. And finally, a major showing at the National Gallery in London. We must remember that at the time of the secretive assessment, two experts refused to comment, and the other expert flat out said that it was not painted by Leonardo.

Jamal Khashoggi is a victim who was silenced via assassination because he was outspoken against his nation of birth. In freer parts of the world, journalists are allowed to be critical of governments and the politicians. The United States, for example, has a wide range of left-wing and right-wing media outlets, and the people operating them have a right to exist without fear of being killed. But freedom to express oneself, and freedom for journalists, is something that is not universally allowed. Khashoggi paid the ultimate price for speaking out. MBS is looking to modernize, and push Saudi Arabia towards a great future. And while he is certainly making impressive strides towards this goal, he is viewed by many people as a brutal dictator. He is also still having to rely on oil for success in his nation.[2] However, for the foreseeable future, he will be able to leverage this to his advantage as the world still depends on oil. But his global public image is something that is needing rehabilitation.

At the time of writing this, the most recent news for the *Salvator Mundi* is that MBS is still creating his museum for the artwork. Simultaneously, more people are beginning to have serious doubts regarding its attribution. The question of how much of a role Leonardo played in its creation is gaining traction. With the artwork being hidden away in the desert, there have been no new scientific examinations of the painting. Furthermore, no one from the art world has come forward with any new, shocking discoveries. News about the *Salvator Mundi* has been relatively quiet but will surely create headlines once again when MBS displays it publicly. And maybe this painting will mark the beginning of Saudi Arabia's plans to try to open themselves up to the rest of the world. As far as this painting goes, what we have is a bad work of art, with a poor provenance, and major attribution issues. The only part of

2. Rundell, "Oil Dependence," line 1.

this image that people can say that Leonardo might have helped with is the blessing right hand. Until now.

There have always been issues regarding the overall appearance of the *Salvator Mundi*. Sure, some of the locks of hair are done with great talent, but there's plenty of contemporaries of Leonardo's that could have painted them. The face itself isn't interesting, in fact it is executed rather poorly. The eyes and jawline are uneven, and the robe does not cast the appropriate shadows. It is also a rather claustrophobic painting. An example is the left thumb being cropped from the canvas because the artist did not use correct proportions. In addition, the walnut panel has a large knot in the middle that ultimately caused it to split. It is hard to imagine da Vinci selecting a subpar panel for his own artwork. A student would more likely be assigned a panel with a knot in it though. These are just a few of the issues with the painting itself, despite there being many more examples. However, people who attribute the *Salvator Mundi* keep going back to the right blessing hand as their leading argument for attribution. Their strongest point is still not even that great of a stance. There is nothing that suggests that Leonardo da Vinci was the only person who could have painted the hand that way. And now there is more information that directly relates to this.

The Massachusetts Institute of Technology (MIT) published a detailed study of the *Salvator Mundi*, and it contains a mind-blowing discovery. MIT used a highly sophisticated software technology system called CNN, which stands for Convolutional Neural Networks. It is a computer program that uses advanced algorithms to discover who the artist behind a particular painting is. This computer system is highlighted as being able to spot forgeries and to help settle attribution disputes. The algorithm displays its results by color coding different parts of the painting. Each color is associated with a degree of certainty that the artist was the person who painted that portion of the work. Red means high likelihood of attribution. Gold is moderate likelihood. Green is moderate likelihood that it was not painted by the given artist. And blue means a high likelihood that the artist did not create that part of the painting. When MIT performed their study, they ran it across the entire artwork. On December 21, 2021, they published their results, and what they found was that their CNN system highlighted the right hand of the *Salvator Mundi* in blue.[3] Before, the strongest case for attribution to da Vinci was the blessing right hand. Now, the most advanced, and unbiased computer system in the world, says that Leonardo da Vinci did not even paint the right hand.

In many ways this story of the *Salvator Mundi* seems to just be getting started. MBS is stuck with the most expensive painting in the world, and many serious scholars do not attribute it to da Vinci. It is doubtful that MBS could even resell the artwork to get his money back. Who would pay $450.3 million for a painting that has such a stigma attached to it? Even if he did resell it, he would still be seen as the gullible prince who fell for a major scam. Some people may still hold on to this attribution, but more and more evidence continues to pile on against these claims. MBS is left with what seems to be only one option, and that is to present the *Salvator Mundi* as an authentic painting by Leonardo da Vinci. Once again when the painting is displayed, there will be another major media campaign to promote it. The forces behind this work will pepper it with impressive, yet irrelevant quotes by historical figures. They will openly talk about how powerful, dynamic, and enigmatic the *Salvator Mundi* is. They will tell fascinating stories about da Vinci and over-romanticize how this painting came to be. And then they will collect their paychecks and keep quiet after their role to play has ended. The brutal truth is that this artwork was never painted by Leonardo. However, it will eventually hang on a wall, behind protective glass, in a beautiful museum. And corrupt powers will continue to shout at us, falsely claiming it was painted by Leonardo da Vinci. This is the Golden Age. Welcome to the circus.

3. Frank and Frank, "Neural Network," lines 26–28.

Bibliography

Aspen Institute. "Martin Kemp, 'The Mona Lisa.'" YouTube, Aug 14, 2017, 57:11. https://www.youtube.com/watch?v=xtYhVk7qsSI.

Auction Podcast. "Martin Kemp, 'Behind the Scenes of Leonardo da Vinci's Salvator Mundi.'" YouTube, Dec 10, 2017, 1:08:32 https://www.youtube.com/watch?v=hMsg7kWge6A.

Bailey, Martin. "Prado Museum Downgrades Leonardo's $450m Salvator Mundi in Exhibition Catalogue." https://www.theartnewspaper.com/2021/11/11/prado-museum-downgrades-leonardos-dollar450m-salvator-mundi-in-exhibition-catalogue.

Bantock, Jack. "Future or Fantasy? Designs Unveiled for One-Building City Stretching 106 Miles in Saudi Arabia". https://www.cnn.com/style/article/saudi-arabia-the-line-city-scli-intl/index.html.

Berger, Miriam. "Former Louvre President Charged in Art Trafficking Case." https://www.washingtonpost.com/world/2022/05/27/louvre-president-jean-luc-martinez-charged-art-trafficking-abu-dhabi/.

Bloomquist, Darin. "The Choiseul Box: A Study of the Duc de Choiseul's Furniture." London: Furniture History Society.

Blostein, Denise. "How a $450 Million da Vinci was Lost in America—and Later Found." https://www.wsj.com/articles/fresh-details-reveal-how-450-million-da-vinci-was-lost-in-americaand-later-found-1537305592.

Brown, Kate. "The Met's Leonardo Expert Says 'Salvator Mundi' was Largely Painted by the Renaissance Master's Assistant." https://news.artnet.com/art-world/carmen-bambach-leonardo-da-vinci-1562602.

Cascone, Sarah. "7 Unbelievable and Contentious Takeaways from a New Documentary about 'Salvator Mundi,' the $450 Million 'Lost Leonardo'". https://news.artnet.com/market/lost-leonardo-salvator-mundi-documentary-2003257.

——— "Is Saudi Arabia Building a Special Museum Just for 'Salvator Mundi'? A Renowned da Vinci Scholar Says It's Already in the Works." https://news.artnet.com/art-world/saudi-arabia-salvator-mundi-museum-2193679.

Charney, Noah. "Chronology of the Mona Lisa: History and Thefts". https://web.archive.org/web/20151027061739/http://blogs.artinfo.com/

secrethistoryofart/2011/08/09/chronology-of-the-mona-lisa-history-and-thefts/.

Chua-Eoan, Howard. "The Top 25 Crimes of the Century". https://web.archive.org/web/20070714103850/http://www.time.com/time/2007/crimes/2.html.

Cole, Alison. "First International Conference on Salvator Mundi: What was the Role of Leonardo's Workshop—and why is Christ Wearing Women's Clothes?" https://www.theartnewspaper.com/2022/11/18/first-international-conference-on-salvator-mundi-what-was-the-role-of-leonardos-workshopand-why-is-christ-wearing-womens-clothes.

———. "How the Louvre Concealed it's Secret Salvator Mundi Book." https://www.theartnewspaper.com/2020/03/31/how-the-louvre-concealed-its-secret-salvator-mundi-book.

———. "Leonardo's Salvator Mundi: Expert Uncovers 'Exciting' New Evidence." https://www.theartnewspaper.com/2018/08/30/leonardos-salvator-mundi-expert-uncovers-exciting-new-evidence.

Conn, David. "Monaco have Plenty of Money and Ambition but Not Many Supporters". https://www.theguardian.com/football/blog/2013/sep/20/monaco-money-ambition-not-many-supporters.

Culotta, Alexis. "The Role of the Workshop in Italian Renaissance Art." https://www.khanacademy.org/humanities/renaissance-reformation/early-renaissance1/beginners-renaissance-florence/a/the-role-of-the-workshop-in-italian-renaissance-art.

Cumming, Robert. *My Dear BB: The Letters of Bernard Berenson and Kenneth Clark, 1925–1959*. New Haven: Yale University Press.

Daley, Michael. "How the Louvre Abu Dhabi Salvator Mundi Became a Leonardo-from-Nowhere." http://artwatch.org.uk/how-the-louvre-abu-dhabi-salvator-mundi-became-a-leonardo-from-nowhere/.

Dalivalle, Margaret and Martin Kemp. *Leonardo's Salvator Mundi & the Collecting of Leonardo in the Stuart Courts*. Oxford: Oxford University Press.

Davis-Marks, Isis. "Art Historian Claims a Newly Discovered Drawing is the Work of Leonardo da Vinci." https://www.smithsonianmag.com/smart-news/did-someone-just-discover-new-leonardo-da-vinci-drawing-1-180976371/.

Edwards, Henry. *Old and New Paris: Its History, Its People, and its Places*. London: Cassell and Co.

Els, Frik. "Two Billionaires Cashed in Big Time Ahead of Uralkali Bombshell". https://www.mining.com/two-billionaires-cashed-in-big-time-ahead-of-uralkali-bombshell-55537/.

Escalante-De Mattei, Shanti. "Long-Lost Rembrandt Painting Found in Italy: 'A Work by a Very Great Author.'" https://www.artnews.com/art-news/news/lost-rembrandt-found-italy-adoration-of-the-magi-1234597041/.

Fedorin, Vladimir. "Dmitry Rybolovlev, Owner of Uralkali. What is the Salt?". https://www.forbes.ru/forbes/issue/2008–05/11470-v-chem-sol.

Bibliography

Fogel, Bryan, dir. *Dissident*. Malibu: Orwell Productions, 2021.

Fontoynont, Marc. "Note on the Revolutionary Lamp Designed to Light Mona Lisa." https://web.archive.org/web/20140829194442/http://www.sbi.dk/indeklima/lys/ny-lampe-til-mona-lisa/Microsoft%20Word%20-%2013-03-Joconde-Summary%20docx%20-2.pdf.

Frank, Robert. "Art Scandal Deepens as 'Stolen' Picassos Surface." https://www.cnbc.com/2015/05/19/did-russian-billionaire-buy-picassos-stepdaughters-stolen-paintings.html

Frank, Steve and Andrea Frank. "A Neural Network Looks at Leonardo's(?) Salvator Mundi. Volume 54, Issue 6." MIT Press Direct, 2021. https://direct.mit.edu/leon/article/54/6/619/97267/A-Neural-Network-Looks-at-Leonardo-s-Salvator.

Graham, August. "Saudi Crown Prince: Murder of Journalist Khashoggi 'Happened on my Watch'". https://www.cityam.com/saudi-crown-prince-murder-of-journalist-khashoggi-happened-on-my-watch/.

Gresham College. "Martin Kemp, 'Leonardo's Salvator Mundi: Scholarship, Science and Skulduggery.'" YouTube, May 13, 2019, 46:08. https://www.youtube.com/watch?v=KIUP8l7HUWI.

Hettie, Judah. "The Men Who Leonardo da Vinci Loved."https://www.bbc.com/culture/article/20191107-the-men-who-leonardo-da-vinci-loved.

Hyatt, John. "What is an Oligarch? Here's What You Need to Know about Russia's Billionaires". https://www.forbes.com/sites/johnhyatt/2022/03/14/what-is-an-oligarch-heres-what-you-need-to-know-about-russias-billionaires/?sh=1e00d87d271f.

Iqbal, Nosheen. "Spiderman's on the Loose! The Art Heists that Shook the World – in Pictures." https://www.theguardian.com/artanddesign/gallery/2009/feb/19/greatest-art-heists-in-pictures.

Isaacson, Walter. *Leonardo da Vinci*. New York: Simon & Schuster, 2017.

Jacobs, Julia. "Christie's Pulls T. Rex from Auction, Citing Need for 'Further Study.'" https://www.nytimes.com/2022/11/20/arts/christies-t-rex-shen-stan.html.

Januszczak, Waldemar. "The Miracle of Da Vinci: Turning a £45 Oddity into a £341m Old Master." https://www.thetimes.co.uk/article/the-miracle-of-da-vinci-turning-a-45-oddity-into-a-341m-old-master-93qzf7gwt.

Kelleher, Suzanne. "Saudi Crown Prince MBS Pressed the Louvre to Lie about His Fake Leonardo Da Vinci, per New Documentary." https://www.forbes.com/sites/suzannerowankelleher/2021/04/09/saudi-crown-prince-mbs-pressed-the-louvre-to-lie-about-his-fake-leonardo-da-vinci-per-new-documentary/?sh=50024a1aed36

Kemp, Martin. *Living with Leonardo*. London: Thames and Hudson, 2018.

Koefoed, Andreas, dir. *The Lost Leonardo*. Hollywood: Sony Pictures, 2021.

Limbong, Andrew. "Artist Peter Doig Says He Didn't Paint This, and a Judge Agrees." https://www.npr.org/sections/thetwo-way/2016/08/23/491024818/judge-to-decide-if-this-painting-is-by-peter-doig-he-says-its-not.

Bibliography

Marani, Pietro. *Leonardo da Vinci: The Complete Paintings*. New York: Harry N. Abrams, 2003.

Modestini, Dianne. "Condition and Restoration." https://salvatormundirevisited.com/Condition-and-Restoration.

——— "History of the *Salvator Mundi*". https://salvatormundirevisited.com/History-of-the-Salvator-Mundi.

——— "Materials and Techniques." https://salvatormundirevisited.com/Materials-Techniques.

Mulholland, Rory. "Monaco FC owner Rybolovlev Among Alleged Victims of Huge Art Scam". https://www.telegraph.co.uk/news/worldnews/europe/monaco/11436640/Swiss-businessman-Yves-Bouvier-arrested-for-art-fraud.html.

Neuendorf, Henri. "Loïc Gouzer on Striking It Out on His Own After a Meteoric Career at Christie's". https://news.artnet.com/art-world/loic-gouzer-interview-1432921.

——— "Who Really Painted 'Salvator Mundi'? An Oxford Art Historian Says it was Leonardo's Assistant." https://news.artnet.com/art-world/did-leonardos-assistant-paint-salvator-mundi-1329638.

New York University: The Institute of Fine Arts. "Dianne Dwyer Modestini." https://ifa.nyu.edu/people/faculty/modestini.htm.

Noce, Vincent. "Antiquities Charges Against Former Louvre Director Could be Dropped." https://www.theartnewspaper.com/2022/11/08/egyptian-antiquities-trafficking-charges-against-former-louvre-director-jean-luc-martinez-and-curator-jean-francois-charnier-could-be-dropped.

Nowinski, Judith. *Baron Dominique Vivant Denon (1747–1825): Hedonist and Scholar in a Period of Transition*. Rutherford, NJ: Fairleigh Dickinson University Press, 1970.

Ottino, Angela. The Complete Paintings of Leonardo da Vinci. London: Penguin, 1986.

Pierpont, Claudia. "The Secret Lives of Leonardo da Vinci." https://www.newyorker.com/magazine/2017/10/16/the-secret-lives-of-leonardo-da-vinci.

Pogrebin, Robin. "Rule-Breaking Rainmaker Leaving Christie's Auction House". https://www.nytimes.com/2018/12/17/arts/design/loic-gouzer-leaving-christies-auction-house.html.

Politics and Prose. "Walter Isaacson, 'Leonardo da Vinci.'" YouTube, Dec 23, 2017, 52:32. https://www.youtube.com/watch?v=mqYJrbmVSoY.

Riding, Alan. "The Louvre's Art: Priceless. The Louvre's Name: Expensive." https://www.nytimes.com/2007/03/07/arts/design/07louv.html.

Rundell, David. "Saudi Arabia Confronts its Oil Dependence". Kleinman Center for Energy Policy, 2022. https://kleinmanenergy.upenn.edu/podcast/saudi-arabia-confronts-its-oil-dependence/#:~:text=Saudi%20Arabia%20is%20the%20world's,foundation%20of%20its%20national%20economy.

Bibliography

Said, Summer, Kelly Crow, and Benoit Faucon. "Record-Setting Leonardo da Vinci Work was Displayed on Saudi Leader's Yacht." https://www.wsj.com/articles/record-setting-leonardo-da-vinci-work-was-displayed-on-saudi-leaders-yacht-11618252319.

Shaheen, Kareem. "They Silenced Khashoggi but Gave Thousands a Voice." https://www.theguardian.com/world/2018/nov/24/jamal-khashoggi-omar-abdulaziz-dissident-saudis-interview.

Small, Zachary. "A Vermeer? It's Actually an Imitator, National Gallery of Art Reveals." https://www.nytimes.com/2022/10/07/arts/vermeer-impostor-national-gallery.html.

Stempel, Jonathan. "Former Twitter Employee is Convicted in Saudi Spy Case". https://www.reuters.com/legal/former-twitter-employee-is-convicted-saudi-spy-case-2022-08-09/.

Stern, Keith. *The Comprehensive Encyclopedia of Historical Gays, Lesbians and Bisexuals, and Transgenders.* Dallas: BenBella Books, 2009.

Tawfeeq, Mohammed. "Jamal Khashoggi's Children 'Pardon' their Father's Killers, Sparing them the Death Penalty." https://www.cnn.com/2020/05/22/middleeast/khashoggi-children-pardon-saudi-intl/index.html.

Thornton, Sarah. "Revealed: $72.8m Rockefeller Rothko has Gone to Qatar." https://www.theartnewspaper.com/article.asp?id=7946.

Torchinsky, Rina. "A Man in a Wig was Detained after Throwing a Piece of Cake at the Mona Lisa". https://www.npr.org/2022/05/30/1102044111/man-throws-cake-at-mona-lisa-the-louvre.

Vilcek, Marica. "Renaissance Woman: Carmen C. Bambach." https://vilcek.org/news/renaissance-woman-carmen-c-bambach/.

Vitkine, Antoine, dir. *Savior for Sale: Da Vinci's Lost Masterpiece?* New York: Greenwich Entertainment, 2021.

Wallace, Robert. *The World of Leonardo: 1452–1519.* Boston, Little Brown & Co., 1966.

Weber, Jasmine. "Major Art Institutions Navigate Ties to Saudi Arabia after Disappearance of Journalist". https://hyperallergic.com/465812/major-art-institutions-navigate-ties-to-saudi-arabia-after-disappearance-of-journalist/.

Worrall, Simon. "What Made Leonardo da Vinci a Genius?"https://www.nationalgeographic.com/history/article/leonardo-da-vinci-genius-walter-Isaacson.

Wright, Margaret. "Copyists at the Louvre." https://www.jstor.org/stable/25627088.

Zöllner, Frank. *Leonardo: The Complete Paintings.* Cologne, Germany: Taschen, 2017.